Also by William C. Ketchum, Jr.

Holiday Ornaments
and Antiques

Holiday Ornaments and Antiques

WILLIAM C. KETCHUM, JR.

with photographs by Schecter Lee

Alfred A. Knopf   New York   1990

THIS IS A BORZOI BOOK
PUBLISHED BY ALFRED A. KNOPF, INC.

Copyright © 1990 by William C. Ketchum, Jr.
Photographs © 1990 by Schecter Lee

Photographs on pages 97, 108. 109, and 114 © Esto Photographics

Library of Congress Cataloging-in-Publication Data
Ketchum, William C., Jr.
Holiday ornaments and antiques / William C. Ketchum, Jr.; with
photographs by Schecter Lee. — 1st ed.
p. cm.
Bibliography: p.
ISBN 0-394-56832-X
1. Holiday decorations — United States — Collectibles. I. Title.
NK805.K469 1989
688.7 — dc19 88-45768
CIP

Manufactured in Hong Kong

FIRST EDITION

OPPOSITE TITLE PAGE: *Halloween cat lantern, made in Germany c. 1920–40.*

Contents

*Porcelain Easter egg cup with chicks, made in either the
United States or Japan c. 1950–60.*

Acknowledgments

I would like to acknowledge with gratitude the following collectors
and institutions whose cooperation was instrumental in the completion
of this book:

Helen and Burt Fendelman, Scarsdale, New York
Brian T. Zompanti, New Britain, Connecticut
Betty and Joel Schatzberg, Greenwich, Connecticut
Gary Davenport, New York, New York
Sharon W. Joel, Jacksonville, Florida
The Margaret Woodbury Strong Museum, Rochester, New York
The Museum of American Folk Art, New York, New York
"Speedy's" Antiques, Greenwich, Connecticut
Nina's Antiques, Portchester, New York

I would also particularly like to express my appreciation
to my good friend Schecter Lee,
who did the photographs used in illustrating the text.

Christmas angel caroller candle, made in the United States c. 1950–60.

Introduction

It is not surprising that collectors should be interested in artifacts associated with important American holidays. What is surprising is that it has taken people this long to become interested in the field. Ten years ago only a handful of people were looking for blown-glass Christmas tree ornaments, papier-mâché Easter bunnies, and creatively painted Halloween masks. Today there are far more enthusiasts, but even they tend to focus on "the big holidays"— Christmas, Halloween, Valentine's Day, and Easter. Events such as New Year's or Mardi Gras that have spawned less-collectible objects or that are not as widely celebrated remain the domain of a relatively limited number of people.

One reason for the increasing popularity of holiday collectibles is that the events with which they are associated touch the lives of almost all of us. Nostalgia tugs at the heart strings when you see the very same set of "Noma" Christmas lights that graced your family's tree for so many years, or a lithographed tin horn identical to the one that used to set your parents' teeth on edge when you blew it at Halloween or on New Year's Eve. It is difficult to think of a collectible category that stirs so many memories for so many.

This interest is already being reflected, unfortunately, in increasing prices, particularly for the more popular objects. It is not unusual for a rare glass ornament dating from the 1920s to bring $100 or more, and the largest turn-of-the-century papier-mâché and plaster-of-Paris Santa Claus figures (12″–20″) may command prices in the low thousands.

Collectors preferring not to pay such prices would do well to focus on less popular collectibles such as those associated with the Thanksgiving and May Day holidays, or on less-sought-after objects relating to the major events. For example, while Dresden and blown-glass Christmas tree ornaments are escalating in value, it is still possible to assemble an interesting collection of ornaments made from cotton batting or spun glass.

Moreover, since this is a relatively young field, one need not buy everything from dealers or at auction. It is still possible to find old holiday items tucked away in an attic (yours or someone else's), or lurking amid a bunch of castoffs at a flea market, yard sale, or even in the local secondhand shop. Christmas and Halloween pieces are especially likely to be found this way, for they have been produced in great numbers and were customarily stored away for reuse.

And, remember, there are no time lines in this field. Some may prefer to collect earlier examples (1920 is considered "early" here); but others will find later and even contemporary pieces interesting. For example, the plastic Christmas bulbs made after World War II are now attracting collector attention, and currently produced Halloween masks are often of high artistic quality.

Collecting rules should be flexible, and both collecting and the collection should be fun. After all, the holidays themselves are for the most part joyous occasions; this joy should be reflected in the hunt for and display of holiday-related objects.

Holiday Ornaments
and Antiques

The New Year's Day dinner is traditional in the United States and most of western Europe. This finely crocheted linen napkin was made in America c. 1900–20, no doubt to grace the table on January 1. The needlework is late Victorian, and the piece measures 5" by 5" when folded. Matching tablecloths are also sometimes found.

New Year's

*T*he ceremonies and celebrations that mark the passing of the old year and the arrival of the new are as varied as the communities observing them. Each reflects the passing of one life cycle and the beginning of another. In the United States, this is seen in the figure of Father Time with his scythe and hourglass, and in the aggressive baby New Year who thrusts him aside at the stroke of twelve.

The annual passing takes place in every culture, but the date in the year varies. Julius Caesar, in 46 B.C., revised the calendar to make January the first month, but even thereafter it was not unusual for New Year's Day to be celebrated at Christmas, in March, or on other dates. The reformation of the Gregorian calendar in the sixteenth century, however, led most Europeans to adopt January 1, though it was not until 1752 that England followed suit.

This uniformity does not prevail in the Eastern world, where New Year's festivities, based on lunar calculations, occur at a different time each year. However, in China, Japan, India, and the Near East the celebrations are no less intense.

Unlike the Orient, the holiday in Occidental countries has little religious significance today, since it is devoted almost exclusively to eating, drinking, dancing, singing, and general merriment—customs that reflect its origins in the ancient winter solstice rites which celebrated the lengthening of the days and the passing of the winter darkness.

The eating of the New Year's dinner may well be traced back to the old Scottish and English custom of Hogmanay, or cake day. On the last day of the

3

year children would go from house to house singing and would be rewarded with oat cakes. A somewhat similar French custom involved the making and giving away of pancakes on New Year's Day.

However, there is more than merriment involved here, for the year's turning has long been regarded as both propitious and foreboding. Father Time himself, with his scythe symbolizing death and destruction and his hourglass marking the unstoppable flow of the years, reminds revelers that their days are numbered. Indeed, Danes believe that if a person peers through the keyhole of a

These lithographed sheet-tin, wood, and plastic clackers or rattles were made c. 1930–70. The use of plastic characterizes the later examples, and the lithographed scenes of merrymaking indicate their relationship to the holiday. Made in the United States; sizes range from 3" to 5".

church on New Year's night, he or she will see before the altar those who are to die in the coming year.

In Maine, people still place a sprig of ivy in a covered dish of water on New Year's Eve and leave it there until Twelfth Night. If the leaf is found fresh and green, one will have a healthy year. But a leaf spotted near the stem means sickness, and one spotted all over means death.

Moreover, the coming year must itself be approached with caution. In northern England it is unlucky to leave the house on the first day of the year until someone has come in. The visitor will bring either good luck or bad. Perhaps in an effort to affect this outcome, it is customary in Scotland to kiss the first person to cross the threshold. On the other hand, in the southern United States it is thought that a wish made on the first white horse seen that day will come true.

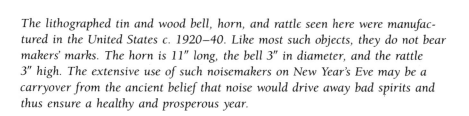

The lithographed tin and wood bell, horn, and rattle seen here were manufactured in the United States c. 1920–40. Like most such objects, they do not bear makers' marks. The horn is 11" long, the bell 3" in diameter, and the rattle 3" high. The extensive use of such noisemakers on New Year's Eve may be a carryover from the ancient belief that noise would drive away bad spirits and thus ensure a healthy and prosperous year.

Types of New Year's Objects

As befits a holiday devoted to eating, drinking, and merrymaking, New Year's collectibles are primarily confined to such items as noisemakers, and the tablecloths and napkins used for the traditional dinner. There is also a variety of greeting cards.

Noisemakers An interesting and extremely varied collection can be built around the noisemakers used in greeting the New Year. These include long, cylindrical horns, clappers consisting of a sheet of metal with a spring-mounted striker on each side, rattles that may be barrel- or mushroom-shaped, and bells or clackers that can produce an exceedingly disagreeable noise by means of an internal ratchet mechanism.

All are made of heavy sheet tin, decorated with lithographed pictures, often of revelers dancing amid showers of confetti and paper streamers. Handles were of wood until the 1950s but are now more often of plastic. The earliest of these devices date from around 1900, but the great majority found today are from the 1920–60 period.

Greeting cards In the nineteenth century, as today, Christmas cards often extended New Year's greetings; there were also those specifically designed for the latter holiday. These were of two kinds, penny-postcards and more ornate examples to be mailed in an envelope (initially at a cost of two cents!). Postcard greetings appeared in Germany in the 1870s but were not popular in the United States until changes in the postal laws in 1898. They remained common from then until the 1920s, when almost entirely replaced by envelope-type cards.

Most popular of the latter are the elaborate pre-1900 cards made in England and, to some extent, in the United States, and the mechanical cards (on one, the

OPPOSITE: *Late-19th- and early-20th-century postcard greetings. The card in the center is from a design by Frances Brundage, one of the most popular of the earlier illustrators. Each greeting is embossed, lithographed cardboard, printed in Germany c. 1910–20.*

This c. 1900–10 New Year's card was made in Germany. The children rolling gold coins symbolizes a wish for wealth in the New Year.

day of the week on which New Year's falls may be changed, so the card can be recycled!) produced in Germany c. 1910–30.

Miscellaneous items Napkins and table coverings used for the traditional New Year's Day dinner were often elaborately crocheted with greetings and, sometimes, with the year or even the guest's name. Such examples are hard to find. For some years now suitably decorated paper napkins and tablecloths have been available, but these are of less interest to collectors than their Halloween counterparts. Despite the gaiety of the occasion, favors and candy boxes associated with it are rare, though there are a few in the form of papier-mâché champagne bottles.

German manufacturers during the late nineteenth and early twentieth centuries produced interesting wall plaques of wax to serve as New Year's greetings. Four to six inches long, decorated with fanciful figures in bright colors, these could be hung from the wall or displayed on a mantel.

Manufacturers

Most sheet-metal noisemakers were produced by American manufacturers. Although the majority are unmarked or simply ink-stamped USA or MADE IN USA or with a patent date or number, it is possible to find examples bearing the names of such well-known toy firms as Marx.

Greeting cards were manufactured during the last years of the past century by such firms as Prang of the United States and Raphael Tuck and Marcus Ward of England. They often marked their cards, and these examples bring a premium. From 1910 until 1940 most of the New Year's cards sold in this country were made in Germany by many companies, including Hildesheimer, Wirth Brothers, and Hogelberg. Makers' names appear, but more often simply GERMANY or PRINTED IN GERMANY.

Valentine's Day

*W**hat*** we now know as Valentine's Day may be traced back to the ancient Roman Lupercalia, a fertility festival held on February 15 and traditionally thought to have been established by the legendary Romulus and Remus. The presiding priests, the Luperci, were devotees of Pan; their rituals, which involved animal sacrifice and symbolic scourging of those within the temple precincts, were designed both to ensure the fertility of earth and mankind and to purify the land for the coming year (February then being the last month of the calendar).

It became customary for young men and women of Rome to exchange scrolls on this date, designating one another sweethearts for the coming year, and to offer each other small gifts. When theirs became the dominant religion, Christians usurped the pagan holidays. Lupercalia, with a calendar adjustment to February 14, became St. Valentine's Day, in commemoration of a third-century martyr. While some pre-Christian elements of the event such as sacrifices were suppressed, the traditions on which our Valentine's Day are based remained.

In medieval England, boys and girls drew lots at St. Valentine's Eve parties to determine couples for the ensuing year, a custom traditionally associated with the mating of birds at this time of the year; and the scraps of paper upon

OPPOSITE: *Valentines generally fall into two broad categories, the sentimental and the comic. Typical of the former is this lithographed, die-cut cardboard and crepe-paper example. This card opens to reveal a lighthouse, symbolizing the light of eternal love, and two children in bucolic dress with a winged cupid to the right. The phrase "Loving Greetings" seen on the card was common during the first part of this century but is seldom used today. Made in Germany c. 1910–30, the piece is 8" tall.*

which names were written gradually evolved into the elaborate valentines of the nineteenth and twentieth centuries. In fact, articles and illustrations from such popular mid-nineteenth-century magazines as *Frank Leslie's Illustrated Newspaper* and *Gleason's Pictorial* make it clear that the holiday as celebrated in 1850 differed little from that of 1950.

But St. Valentine's Day also had a different, darker face. The expressions of love, devotion, and admiration typical of most cards were contrasted with those of ridicule and slander set forth in the so-called comic valentines. We do not know how old the latter are, but as far back as 1868 *Godey's Lady's Book* contained a drawing of a schoolmaster receiving such a nasty missive.

While exchange of greeting cards is the central element of the day, St. Valentine's is also a time for gift giving and for prophecy of marriage prospects. Today, candy is the usual token; but in the 1870s acceptable gifts included fans, hairpins, pincushions, brooches, watches, lockets, rings, music boxes, silk neckties, and embroidered slippers.

Comic valentines have existed since at least the 18th century. Often designed to wound rather than to flatter, in former times they might lead to duels or other violent acts. In this simple mechanical valentine, pulling on the little boy causes the young lady to rise from a battered garbage can. The lithographed, die-cut card is marked PRINTED IN GERMANY *and was produced there c. 1925–35.*

To my ♡♥ Valentine

PRINTED IN GERMANY.

This lithographed, die-cut cardboard and crepe-paper card was made in Germany c. 1910–20, but note the ship flies an American flag, indicating the piece was made for sale in this country. A sizable example, it is roughly 10″ square.

BELOW: *Cut crepe paper, which could fold flat for mailing and then open out to create a three-dimensional card, was employed in most better-quality greetings. Here it is combined with two lithographed, die-cut, cardboard cupids, both of whom are holding ivy vines. Since these entwine and embrace any plant or object they come into contact with, they are closely associated with the mythology of Valentine's Day. The illustrated card is 9″ high and was manufactured in Germany between 1920 and 1930.*

OPPOSITE: *The moon appears frequently in valentine composition—no doubt not only because lovers frequent the moonlight but also because among some people a wish made on the moon if not revealed will come true. The laurel pictured in this card reflects the fact that this plant is known as a love charm. In England it is thought that if a person places two laurel leaves on the pillow, he or she will dream of love. Made from lithographed, die-cut cardboard and crepe paper, this example was manufactured in Germany around 1925–35. It is 11″ tall.*

Types of Valentine's Day Collectibles

Since neither elaborate meals nor extensive gift giving are now associated with the holiday, valentine-related items are confined primarily to a single category, that of greeting cards. However, other objects such as candy boxes (primarily heart-shaped), magazine and newspaper articles dealing with the event, and the various molds used to shape valentine cakes and candies offer interesting possibilities for the enthusiast.

Greeting cards Valentines are by far the most complex and artistic of greeting cards, as well as the oldest. As far back as the eighteenth century the London firm of Kershaw, Canton & Lloyd was turning out elaborate hand-cut and -painted examples; and during the nineteenth and early twentieth centuries many firms—English, German, and American—catered to a public taste for beauty and novelty.

The cards they produced were by modern standards remarkable. The traditional motifs of flowers, laurel leaves, birds, the lute and other musical instruments, outstretched hands, and, of course, Cupid were combined with mirror glass, silvered paper frames, crepe paper, silk, and muslin to create a form of miniature theater. In fact, during the late 1800s it was not unusual for the feathers of exotic birds and even these very birds, stuffed and boxed in tiny nests, to be utilized in the more costly missives. Hummingbirds, carefully prepared by nuns in Brazilian convents, were a particular favorite!

The February 1876 edition of *St. Nicholas* magazine describes the making of these better-quality cards in some detail, noting that to the lithographed cardboard background was added a die-cut lace pattern, and then the central design was hand-tinted by young women working in what was essentially a small factory. Ribbons, bits of glass, feathers, and other embellishments were then glued on. The cost of such ephemera could vary greatly. In 1875, one London firm produced 368 different valentine types. The least expensive cost two cents, but the most extravagant were sold for $60, an incredible sum at a time when most workingmen made $10–15 per week.

The earlier cards favored romantic bowers and courtship scenes; however, by the 1900s the traditional lovers had been "transported" by new means— ships, locomotives, motorcars, and even airplanes. Moreover, where Victorian

The American romance with the railways led to a variety of valentines featuring trains or locomotives. This foldout card is made of lithographed, die-cut card-board and silver gilt. Cupid as an engineer drives this latter-day version of the classic chariot of love. The abundance of spring flowers embellishing the loco-motive reflects the association of this holiday with the coming of spring. The card is 11" long and was manufactured in Germany around 1920–30.

valentines featured adults, the protagonists of many c. 1910–40 cards were children who assumed adult roles. The traditional lacy foldout cards were also supplemented by interesting mechanical pop-up ones. Both types are popular with contemporary collectors.

Candy boxes The heart-shaped boxes in which valentine sweets come are now attracting some attention. Made of cardboard, often covered with flocking or silver foil embellished with ribbons of silk or satin, and ranging in size from a few inches to more than a foot across, these can form the basis of an interesting collection.

This realistic representation of an early-20th-century touring car opens to a fully developed three-dimensional vehicle mounted on four wheels. Manufactured in Germany c. 1910–20, the piece is 10″ long and made of lithographed, die-cut cardboard.

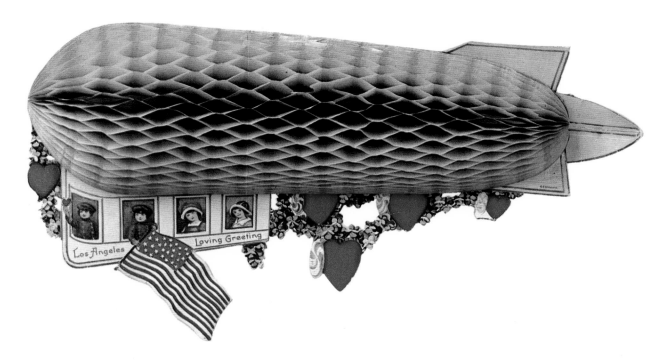

Early valentines were more than just greeting cards. This foldout dirigible—made of accordion-pleated crepe paper and lithographed, die-cut cardboard—also serves as a promotional device for the city of Los Angeles, whence come "Loving Greetings." The piece was made in Germany c. 1920–30. Larger than most, this card is 12" long.

LEFT: *Art Deco motifs date this unusual card to the 1930s. Made of crepe paper and lithographed, die-cut cardboard, the piece was manufactured in Germany. The airplane (a biplane since it has two wings) appears frequently on valentines of this period, here combined with doves, the winged messengers of love. Some 7" high, the piece is marked* PRINTED IN GERMANY.

RIGHT: *The lighthouse, whose beacon in the dark symbolizes salvation for the lost, provides an interesting background for this boatload of valentine revelers. The printed message on the reverse mirrors the stormy seas of romance: "To my Valentine. I want to send a Valentine,/ A pretty one to you;/But it takes a lot of courage./Such a bold, bold thing to do." German, c. 1915–30, made of lithographed, die-cut cardboard, and 11" high.*

Not all friends and lovers confined themselves to commercially made tokens. This chip-carved, heart-shaped tramp-art box was made in the United States c. 1900–20 of cigar-box mahogany. The top swivels to the side to reveal a recess that could be filled with sweets or trinkets. The box is 5″ long.

Miscellaneous items

Occasionally one will find handcrafted objects associated with St. Valentine's. One such example, shown here, is a tramp-art box in the shape of a heart. It may have been used to store candy or even a bottle of perfume. Other rare gifts of the day include hooked rugs and quilts with a heart motif and tiny heart-shaped pincushions cut out of cotton scraps.

In some homes it was traditional to prepare a St. Valentine's sponge cake that would be baked in a tin heart-form mold and covered with pink frosting. Cookies might be pressed into carved wooden molds or punched out with a similarly shaped tin cutter. Most interesting of all are those molds that feature the heart within an open hand, an ancient European device symbolic of giving one's hand in marriage. Most of these items date to the nineteenth century, and none are easy to find today.

Manufacturers

Valentine cards were turned out in great quantities by numerous English, German, and American manufacturers, but the lack of identifying marks makes it impossible to identify most. However, substantial numbers of marked cards do exist. Among the better-known producers are McLoughlin Brothers of New York City (c. 1850–1920), Raphael Tuck & Company of London and Paris (1868–), F. Priester & Eyck, Berlin (c. 1870–1916), Louis Prang & Company, Boston (c. 1874–90), and Marcus Ward (c. 1872–97), who commissioned much of the work done by the popular illustrator Kate Greenaway. Signed Greenaway cards (she designed over a hundred) bring a premium with most collectors.

The Valentine's Day table was often graced by a large heart-shaped cake that could have been prepared in this sheet-tin mold. Measuring 10" by 12", this example was made in New England c. 1840–70. Similar though perforated molds were used in Pennsylvania to shape cottage cheese.

The so-called stand-up valentines, which open up to form a base, were produced c. 1895–1935 by various German manufacturers, but other than the ubiquitous GERMANY or PRINTED IN GERMANY, they were seldom identified.

Candy boxes were made both in the United States and in Germany. At present collectors are less interested in the identity of the maker than the rarity or artistic quality of the box; and, in any case, most are unidentified.

The same is true of the one-of-a-kind, folk-art objects identified with the holiday such as molds, cookie cutters, and quilts.

The giving of small gifts of candies or sweets on Valentine's Day has long been an American tradition. Seen here is a wooden mold made of pine and measuring 12" by 20". It was used in the making of heart-shaped gingerbread cookies. Pennsylvania, c. 1820–50.

Easter

*T*he modern Easter combines the Christian festival commemorating the resurrection of Christ with the remnants of ancient pagan rites celebrating the rebirth of spring. It also coincides with the Jewish holiday of Pesach, or Passover. Falling on the Sunday after the first full moon on or following March 21, Easter is a joyous holiday combining religious services with more secular customs such as the display of finery in the "Easter Parade" and the various traditions surrounding the fertility symbols of egg and rabbit. It is to the latter that we owe the numerous Easter novelties.

Much of the lore associated with the egg and the Easter Bunny may be traced to Germany, where pagan tribes regarded the egg as the symbol of life's beginning and its yolk and white as the sun and moon. Moreover, it was the rabbit who served as escort to the Teutonic goddess Ostara, whose name in an altered form became that of the festival, Easter.

The custom of hiding and then hunting for decorated eggs originated in the United States, as did the Easter Egg Roll in which children competed to see how far downhill their eggs could be propelled—a tradition still carried out on the lawn of the White House in Washington, D.C.

As early as 1680, the children of Germanic immigrants in Pennsylvania were putting out their caps and bonnets on Easter eve that they might be filled with eggs by the Easter Bunny, while their elders vied to see who could eat the

OPPOSITE: *Finely crafted plaster-of-Paris rabbit candy containers such as these were manufactured in Germany during the 1920s and 1930s. They range in height from 3.5" to 5.5", and all open at neck or waist so that candy may be stored within.*

most "cackle berries," or hard-boiled eggs. Another contest, popular in the southern United States, is "nicking," wherein two children rap their eggs together until one cracks. The owner of the undamaged egg then appropriates that of his opponent.

Other old Easter customs that have fallen into disuse include dipping the *Osterwasser* (Easter water), which is scooped against the current and thought to have curative properties; the sacrifice of the Easter lamb; the telling of jokes, *Ostermarchen;* and strangest of all, the "Easter Smacks," mild whippings with green boughs administered in turn by men to women and women to men on Easter Monday and Easter Tuesday. It was thought that these would preserve youth, bring good luck and health, and protect from vermin.

Types of Easter Souvenirs

The bulk of Easter collectibles relate in some way to either eggs or rabbits; however, other animal forms such as lambs, chickens, and ducks are found, and there are more toys than are associated with any other holiday except Christmas.

Candy containers The Germans have given candy as an Easter present for hundreds of years; in 1853, they created the first *Osterhasen,* or Easter Bunny container, for this. Made of papier-mâché cast in halves, then glued together and hand-painted in oils, these pieces were the forerunners of the many such containers produced for Halloween, Christmas, and other occasions.

Designed in three positions—standing, sitting, and walking—the first rabbits were 3″ to 16″ high and be could separated at the neck or middle to allow

As the central figure of the Easter tradition, the egg- and candy-bearing rabbit assumed many costumes. This 10″-tall, papier-mâché example is dressed like a proper European businessman. He was produced in Germany c. 1920–35.

26

for the insertion of sweets. In time the traditional form was supplemented, sometimes by a basket in which jelly eggs could be carried, and in other instances by the addition of costumes as varied as those of baseball players, chauffeurs, and rustic characters.

After 1900, other materials were also used. Plaster of Paris was popular because it could be molded with great detail and took paint well, while pasteboard figures introduced in the 1930s were less costly. The Japanese entered the field in the thirties with celluloid; and after World War II, they, the Taiwanese, and Hong Kong manufacturers converted to plastic, which has yet to capture the imagination of collectors.

In 1870, German firms introduced the first egg-form containers. These *Ostereiers,* or Easter eggs, were made of compressed pasteboard covered with lithographed scenes and separated in the center so that they might be filled with sugar candies. There had, however, been earlier Easter egg novelties. In the mid-nineteenth century egg-shaped milk glass "blanks" sold by glass manufacturers were oil-painted in bright colors, usually by amateur or "Sunday" painters. Then, in 1883, Alexander III, Czar of Russia, contracted with the goldsmith Peter Carl Fabergé for the first of what were to become the world's most costly Easter novelties. Gilded, enameled, and jewel-covered eggs, usually containing mechanical elements, were made until the collapse of the Russian Empire in 1917. Today, these and other Fabergé eggs sell for prices that make their collecting prohibitive for all but a few. Much more reasonably priced are the two-piece lithographed tin eggs which supplemented the earlier papier-mâché ones during the early 1900s.

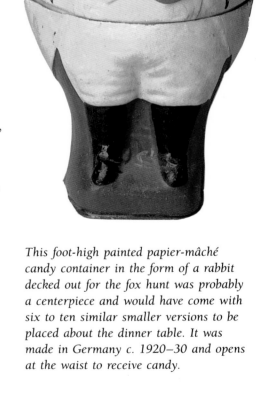

This foot-high painted papier-mâché candy container in the form of a rabbit decked out for the fox hunt was probably a centerpiece and would have come with six to ten similar smaller versions to be placed about the dinner table. It was made in Germany c. 1920–30 and opens at the waist to receive candy.

Representative of a new form of rabbit candy container, this pressed pasteboard example was introduced in 1935 by the German firm of Emil Stauch. Production was terminated during World War II. This piece is 7″ high and stamped GERMANY. *Its ears end in wire springs and will jiggle when the rabbit is moved.*

Though not particularly common, other early-twentieth-century candy container forms can be found. In the 1920s and 30s popular cartoon and advertising figures like Snookums, Foxy Grandpa, the Palmer Cox Brownie, and the Campbell Soup Kid appeared in the United States in this guise, as well as ducks, roosters, chicks, and pigs. Many of these were plaster-of-Paris nodding figures with heads mounted on coiled springs.

Toys There are quite a few German, American, and Japanese toys with an Easter theme. Groups of papier-mâché rabbits doubled as ninepins to be used in a simple bowling game, while others were mounted on wheeled platforms as pull toys, or themselves pulled candy- or egg-laden wooden carts. There are also mechanical toys, including such items as an American-made, lithographed tin hen which lays colored wooden eggs and clucks when a crank is turned, a Japanese plastic and tin rabbit on a tricycle, and a late-nineteenth-century French automaton consisting of a rabbit driving a primitive auto. As the steel spring unwinds, the rabbit propels his vehicle in a figure-eight pattern and raises and lowers the spectacles held in his hand. And there are a few walking wind-up toys, such as a duck dressed in peasant costume who waddles along carrying her basket of jelly eggs.

Though they had previously been active in the field, Japanese manufacturers entered the Easter novelty business in a big way during the 1950s. Since then they have produced many pieces, such as this lithographed tin and plastic wind-up toy which measures 4″ by 6″ and was made in the 1960s.

ABOVE: *Hens and chicks run a distant second to the rabbit as Easter symbol. However, when you turn the handle, this lithographed tin hen lays colorful wooden Easter eggs! Measuring 5″ by 5.5″, the piece was made and marked by the Baldwin Manufacturing Co. of Brooklyn, New York, c. 1950–55.*

OPPOSITE: *This cast-iron Easter Bunny was designed to be used as a doorstop. It is 9″ high and was manufactured in the United States c. 1910–30.*

Easter baskets come in many shapes and sizes, all collectible. This stained-splint example is only 4″ high. It is marked JAPAN *on the base. The three chicks are of cotton wool and less than 2″ tall. Made in Japan c. 1950–60.*

Easter baskets During the late nineteenth and early twentieth centuries many Easter baskets of splint, willow, or reed were made in Germany and the United States. These were usually dyed (as with the splint examples made by the Penobscot Indians of Maine and Nova Scotia) or decorated with ribbons and bits of brightly colored paper. Less common are the German baskets made from knitted wool soaked in sugar water and allowed to harden, then filled with shredded green or purple "grass" cut from wax paper. Small rolled and dyed cotton rabbits and chicks with wire feet were put in the baskets.

Decorated eggs The custom of decorating eggshells originated in eastern Europe and is now popular in the United States. Uncooked eggs are emptied of their contents by blowing the yolk and white out of holes drilled in the ends. The shells are then painted with oils or watercolors and, sometimes, embellished with beadwork and découpage. The result is attractive but extremely fragile. Somewhat more durable are the spun-sugar eggs that have been produced in Europe since the turn of the century. These often are made with an interior view of a lithographed, die-cut scene, or small three-dimensional figures. In 1971 these were supplemented by the first hollow porcelain Easter eggs. Made in limited editions with the collector in mind, porcelain eggs are now produced by many well-known manufacturers, including Limoges, Noritake, and Wedgwood.

Greeting cards Easter greeting cards, both penny-postal type and envelope-enclosed forms, have been produced by English, American, and German printing houses since before 1900. Although many have religious themes that are not popular with collectors, some feature humorous versions of rabbits, chicks, and the like. These are sought both by Easter specialists and by general greeting-card collectors.

Manufacturers

The earliest known maker of Easter candy containers was the Emil Stauch Company of Unterrdach, Germany, which started producing them in 1853, employing the usual "cottage industry" method of farming the work out to families in the Thuringia region. Rabbits were made first, and eggs were introduced in 1870. By 1900, other firms such as Max Denner and Grempel & Handel of Kronach had joined the field. In 1920, Hermann Wirth of Neustadt produced sitting, standing, and walking rabbits, each in twenty-four sizes ranging from 3″ to 16″ and selling (usually through bakeries and candy stores) for one to twenty-five cents apiece. Unfortunately, few of these pieces are individually marked, other than the simple GERMANY or MADE IN GERMANY. The cardboard shipping containers bore more information, but they are seldom found today.

Competition for the German manufacturers came during the 1920s and 30s when Japanese shops turned out rather garish papier-mâché pieces and when an American firm, Pulp Productions of Milwaukee, Wisconsin, introduced a line of paper-pulp rabbits stained white and decorated in blue, green, yellow, or pink.

Although papier-mâché or plaster-of-Paris toys were often made by the same firms that made candy containers, lithographed tin toys were usually produced by large toymakers as a sideline or specialty. The best-known German manufacturer was Ernest Paul Lehmann of Brandenburg (now Nuremberg), Germany, established in 1881. The company's logo, E.P.L., often appears on Easter playthings such as the clockwork "Chanticleer Cart," which features a rooster pulling a two-wheeled wagon on which a rabbit sits. Since Lehmann toys in general are costly, the few with an Easter theme bring a premium.

American manufacturers include Louis Marx & Company of New York City (1921–76) and the Baldwin Manufacturing Company of Brooklyn, New York, designer of the "Little Red Hen" toy. Both Marx and Baldwin Easter toys are always marked. Other American-made Easter toys may be stamped USA or MADE IN USA or bear a patent date or number.

Post-1950 mechanical toys with an Easter theme have been made in Japan, Taiwan, and Hong Kong. Some list only country of origin, though others may be stamped with a maker's name. At present, collectors do not show the same interest in objects by these companies as they do in those produced by Marx or Lehmann.

These Easter cards were made in Germany c. 1900–20. Note the quaint greeting, quite different from present day Easter salutations.

35

Halloween

Halloween is primarily thought of as a children's holiday. The event has a long and complex history, and many of the items associated with it reflect a time when the celebration was universal and of great importance to the community. "Trick-or-treat" masks and costumes, noisemakers, and the involvement of ghosts, witches and the Devil all reflect ancient beliefs and practices largely forgotten now.

Halloween or All Halloweven, October 31, is the amalgam of two ancient holidays—All Hallows or All Saints' Day, and Samain. The former, a date commemorating the deaths of saints and martyrs, was introduced in the seventh century by Pope Boniface IV to supplant the ancient pagan festival of the dead. Samain, its origins lost in antiquity, was a harvest festival whose purpose was to give thanks for the year's production and to assure a bountiful one in the coming season.

The history and customs of both events are mirrored in the symbolism of present-day Halloween. Central to the festival of the dead was the fear that legions of the departed would arise on this night to do harm to the living, and the consequent desire to propitiate these restless spirits.

In much of Europe "soul cakes," gingerbread or sweet tarts, were especially

OPPOSITE: *Probably once an andiron or doorstop, this 15″-high sheet-iron cat shows traces of old paint. It was handmade in the United States in the early 1900s. Not all superstitions surrounding the cat are necessarily bad. In Japan, the "beckoning cat" is placed in a shop window to draw trade; and in New England, it is thought that you can tell the time of day by the size of a cat's pupils. Eastern Canada has a parallel belief that the animal's pupils vary in size depending on the height of the tide.*

baked to be left on graves for the sustenance of the hungry dead or given to the poor as proxies for them. More relevant to modern Halloween customs was the old English tradition of children who went "a-souling" from house to house, singing songs and receiving soul cakes in return. In many homes the sweets would be piled upon a plate and visitors would be urged to eat while family members sang: "A soul cake, a soul cake; have mercy on all Christian souls for a soul cake." One or more of the cakes would contain a ring or a coin, and it was thought that whoever found the coin would grow prosperous. In South America, skulls molded of sugar took the place of the cakes.

Samain too served as an antecedent for contemporary trick or treaters, for the traditional harvest festival was preceded by scavenging expeditions organized by groups of horn-blowing youths, who would go from farm to farm gathering food and money for the coming festivities. But it also had a darker side, for it was at this time that the ancient Druids of Ireland sacrificed their human victims, and many also thought that on this day child-stealing demons or samhanach (witches) rose from their barrows to roam the world.

Although fragments of these ancient ceremonies can still be found in parts of Europe and the Americas, only in the United States has the holiday become one of unrestrained merrymaking, characterized by children's parades, costume balls, parties, and, of course, the ritualized beggary of trick or treat.

By the 1920s Halloween parties had become big business, providing a lucrative income to manufacturers supplying everything from costumes and masks to candy, party favors, and disposable paper plates, napkins, and tablecloths. One firm, the Dennison Manufacturing Company of Framingham, Massachusetts, advertised in 1930 the following list of "ready made helps for the Halloween hostess": gummed seals, cardboard cutouts, invitations, place cards, score cards, crepe paper, paper napkins, paper table covers, streamers, festoons, crepe-paper moss, serving cups, and hall decorations.

There was even a magazine, *Parties,* devoted to providing parents (exclusively mothers in those days) with helpful hints on how to arrange, stock, and successfully conduct a Halloween party. The Fall 1930 edition of *Parties* provides a complete scenario for a Halloween bash that seems more suited to adults or teenagers than to children.

After discussing suitable invitations, the article describes various moneymaking games designed to help the party pay for itself. Chief among these is "The Witches' Wood," which features a suitably attired crone who, if one threw a coin into her boiling cauldron, would foretell the future from leaves plucked from an artificial tree. Suggested fates indicate much about preoccupa-

While the piercing eyes, fanglike teeth and wart-marked face seen here are a common characterization of the Halloween witch, the form is unusual. In most areas of the United States fans are not needed at the end of October, and very few such examples are associated with Halloween. This highly artistic one is made of lithographed and crepe paper and is 7″ high. Made in Germany, the piece dates to about 1920.

The warlock, like the witch, had extensive powers of transformation, divination, invulnerability to most illnesses, accidents, and weapons, and the capacity to create charms and spells that could control the fates of normal human beings. However, in an interesting comment on the feminist theme, the warlock was seldom either as powerful or as much a figure of folklore as the witch. Here his face appears on a painted plaster and paper lantern made in Germany c. 1900–10. That the warlock appears to be emerging from a tree trunk possibly reflects both the naturalistic Art Nouveau taste of the period and the wizard's shape-changing skills. The piece is 6″ high by 6.5″ in diameter.

tions of the time, as well as traditional word plays: "Ash-vain hopes, Lemon-unhappy marriage, Pear-marry soon, Cherry-you will join the Reds [i.e., Communist Party]."

Most of the fortunes are concerned with marriage prospects, a fascinating coincidence since some of the earliest Halloween beliefs center on the same area of life. For example, in Wales it was thought that if on Halloween night a young woman walked backward to an onion plot in the kitchen garden and left a knife on the ground there, she would have a vision of her future husband, who would pick up the blade and cast it from the garden. And in Ireland, maidens sowed hemp seed on the holiday, believing that if in the process they looked behind them, they would see the shadow of a coming spouse.

Types of Halloween Collectibles

With the exception of Christmas, no holiday can compare with this one in the variety of interesting objects. There are masks and costumes, a selection of lanterns, noisemakers, trick-or-treat bags, toys, greeting cards, favors including candy boxes and various table, mantel, and room decorations, as well as a few cookie cutters and candy molds.

Masks and costumes Masks and costumes are inherently fragile, and few of any age have survived. Made primarily of printed or hand-painted cotton gauze stiffened with sizing, they are not currently of great interest to most collectors. However, the child who goes forth on Halloween night clad as Batman or Caspar the Ghost is engaging in an ages-old ritual. Masks disguise, conceal, and transform the wearer, hiding him or her from enemies, striking fear into them, and, in the ideal sense, identifying the wearer with the character personified, endowing him with its strength and virtue.

Thus, in ancient Ireland, the Halloween procession was headed by a man called the White Mare who wore a white robe and semblance of a horse's head, while in Scotland costumed mummers sought alms for the festivities.

The earliest costumes recalled local deities or sacred animals, or mimicked (and thus repelled) feared antagonists such as the Devil, witches, and the undead; contemporary costumes run the gamut of modern life from rock stars and patriotic or political figures to comic-strip heroes and perennial children's favorites such as the Good Fairy and Snow White. While subject to special

ABOVE: *Witch-form weathervanes such as the one seen here are uncommon. The form is associated with a single day in the year; even today in this country there are those who believe in and fear witches and the idea of a witch riding the sky above their house or barn would be quite unacceptable. This painted sheet-iron vane is American, 19″ by 17″, and dates from c. 1900–20. Unlike most Halloween objects, which are factory made, this was handcrafted.*

OPPOSITE: *This simple musical instrument measures 4″ by 7″ and was made in Germany in the 1930s. It is made of wood, lithographed paper, and cardboard.*

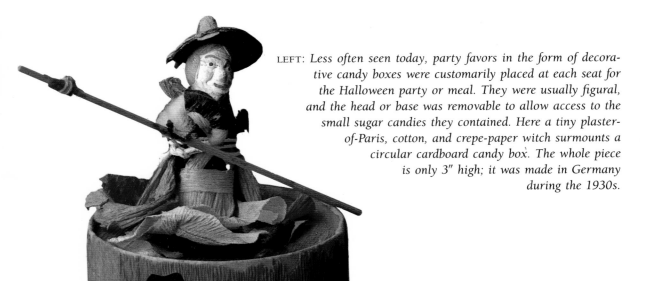

LEFT: *Less often seen today, party favors in the form of decorative candy boxes were customarily placed at each seat for the Halloween party or meal. They were usually figural, and the head or base was removable to allow access to the small sugar candies they contained. Here a tiny plaster-of-Paris, cotton, and crepe-paper witch surmounts a circular cardboard candy box. The whole piece is only 3" high; it was made in Germany during the 1930s.*

RIGHT AND OPPOSITE: *Noisemakers have a curious relationship to the Halloween holiday. Clackers or rattles —such as the two wooden, crepe-paper, and painted plaster-of-Paris examples seen here—are for us a source of amusement (or annoyance) in the hands of youthful revelers. However, during the Middle Ages it was believed that noise would drive away evil spirits, and rattles like these were also carried in religious processions by members of the Penitente cults of Spain and South America. The illustrated examples are 4" and 6" high, respectively, and were manufactured c. 1920–30. Both are marked* GERMANY.

problems in display and preservation, masks and costumes offer an exciting new field for the collector.

Lanterns Traditionally used both to light the way for revelers and to serve as a beacon to encourage would-be trick or treaters, lanterns are found in a great many shapes and sizes. The pumpkin form is often referred to as a jack-o'-lantern as its flickering light was formerly thought to resemble the will-o'-the-wisp or fox fire, phosphorescent light caused by rotting vegetation.

Even today most lanterns are candle-lit (sometimes by choice, as in Arkansas where some still believe that a lighted candle protects against a witch's spells); however, late-nineteenth-century makers experimented with kerosene, and since 1960 various battery-operated examples have appeared. By far the finest are the lanterns molded from papier-mâché and painted in a highly naturalistic manner. Whether pumpkins, witches, cats, or devils, these are among the most artistic and most sought after of Halloween collectibles. Most date from c. 1900–40.

Lanterns made of lithographed sheet tin or cardboard or even of the highly flammable tissue paper may be found; and in recent years molded plastic has become popular, though both design and color are mediocre.

OPPOSITE TOP: *The commonplace appearance of cats in Halloween memorabilia, either as companions to witches or alone, reflects the importance this animal bears in the mythology of the holiday. At least since the time of the Egyptians, cats have played the dual role of pet and demigod. Even today there are those who believe that they have special powers. Some fear that to kill a cat is to invite its posthumous vengeance; while for others, merely to kick the beast may result in an attack of rheumatism. The haunting, wide-eyed stare of the cat is frequently mimicked in Halloween lanterns where candlelight causes the eyes to glow in an almost too-realistic manner. The three cat-head lanterns illustrated here range in size from 3.5" to 5" and were all made in Germany c. 1910–25. Those at left and right are of papier-mâché, while the one in the middle, which reverses to show an owl's head, is of plaster.*

BELOW: *Candy containers are among the most popular of Halloween collectibles. Though made in small factories, they were carefully hand-molded and painted, as here, in order to create humorous, doll-like forms. Since World War II, high labor costs have prohibited the manufacture of such novelties. The two witches illustrated are accompanied by a pumpkin man. All three were produced in Germany c. 1920–30 and are of plaster of Paris. The witches have cardboard hats and straw or paper hair; height 4–7".*

RIGHT: *For some Americans the black cat is a witch in transformation, a hoodoo, or even the Devil himself, and is capable of bringing death or misfortune. This supposed power has often worked to the animal's disadvantage. In parts of the South, broth made from a black cat is thought to cure consumption, while members of certain religious cults employ cats' eyes and hair in charms and fetishes. This 9″ cat candy container, large for his type, is of papier-mâché and wears a crepe-paper bow tie. It is from Germany and dates to the 1930s.*

As the adversary of God and the personification of all evil, Satan or the Devil customarily appears, as in the illustrated crepe-paper lantern, in the form of a handsome but sinister man, with slanting eyes, pointed ears, and prominent eyebrows. However, his true character is more often evidenced by the horns on his forehead, a pointed tail, bat's wings, and a cloven foot. For those who miss these clues there is always the smell of hellish brimstone. The Devil's proclivity for mischiefmaking is evident in this flimsy folding lantern. Any parent who allowed a child to place a lighted candle in it would be courting disaster. Made in the United States c. 1940, the lantern is 8″ in diameter.

Noisemakers Noise is synonymous with Halloween, whether the long-drawn-out "whoooo" of the pint-sized ghost or the whistling, banging, and honking produced by a variety of factory-made instruments. And it has long been thus. Since witches, spooks, and even Old Nick himself have never been partial to loud sounds, those traveling abroad at night, particularly on All Hallows Eve, have made a point of creating enough ruckus to drive the demons from their path.

During this century, Halloween "music" has been employed in a somewhat different but equally coercive manner. What householder, confronted by a band of tin horns, rattles, and whistles, would not gladly dole out candy and pennies for a bit of peace and quiet?

The majority of collectible noisemakers are of tin and wood. There are lithographed tin horns (often vaguely resembling a witch's hat), whistles and bells of similar construction, and wooden clackers whose ingenious construction incorporates various figures such as witches, cats, and the like. Less common are primitive accordions of wood and paper, and highly stylized rattles whose pumpkin faces have the stark quality of African art.

Trick-or-treat bags A recent innovation and very much a sign of the times is the designer trick-or-treat bag. Until twenty or thirty years ago, it was quite acceptable for children to stuff their goodies into a plain brown paper sack. However, it is now possible to buy specially designed ones featuring Halloween motifs and such lettering as TRICK OR TREAT or the hardly subtle GIVE. Some of the more graphic of these bags are already being mounted under glass as wall decorations.

Toys There are few true toys associated with Halloween, though one will occasionally encounter wooden jumping jacks in the form of witches or pumpkin heads, or a jack-in-the-box that opens to reveal a cat or witch. Much

Referred to in German folk tales as *gute, dumme Teufel,* or the good, dumb
Devil, he is often outwitted by humans whom he attempts to lead astray.
Indeed, most Halloween representations of Satan are humorous rather than
foreboding. Here he appears as a squat, snaggle-toothed imp whose function is
to serve as a party favor and candy box. His odd garb may be explained as a
matter of industrial practicality. Old Nick and his messenger, the cat, have bodies cast in identical molds; they were just painted differently. Both were made in
Germany c. 1920–35, of papier-mâché.

The concept of death, personified here by a shrouded and ghostlike skull, is very much a part of the Halloween tradition and has a long history in western Europe. The lithographed paper, crepe-paper, and wood rattle seen here was presented as a dance favor at a party in the fall of 1927. It is 8″ high including the handle, and is German in origin.

Death personified as a witch is an unusual though not unknown concept, combining the symbol of doom with one who could bring it. This figure, only 4″ high, was probably an ornament or party favor. As such pieces go, it is fairly complex, combining a wire-spring and cloth body with plaster-of-Paris head, hands, and feet, and a hand-carved wooden broom. It was produced in Germany during the 1930s.

This is a rare variation on the numerous small outhouse figures made in this country and abroad during the early 1900s. Composed of papier-mâché and pipe cleaners, the skeletal figure sits within a pine privy 4" high. It was made in Germany c. 1920–40.

The appearance of skeletons in the Halloween parade is closely linked to the ancient belief that the bones are the residence of the physical soul (as opposed to the spiritual one) and that if possessed of sufficient vitality or if sufficiently angry at the living, these will rise up, not only to walk but to wreak destruction. To prevent this, a stake was often driven through the body of an executed witch or criminal, and the "bone fire" (which became "bonfire") was used to destroy potentially dangerous bodies. The articulated plaster-of-Paris figure shown here is 5" tall and strung on wire. It was probably a favor or an ornament. It is German, c. 1900–20.

harder to come by are mechanical playthings such as a walking, clockwork ghost or a sparkler toy. In the latter, turning a handle causes a metal ratchet to scrape across flint or sandpaper, creating a sparking effect that is seen through the celluloid- or paper-covered eyes of a devil, cat, or pumpkin.

Favors and candy boxes From late Victorian times to the present it has been customary to mark each place at the Halloween table with a favor, a small figure of a witch, cat, pumpkin, owl, devil, and so on, which is a gift to the holiday guest. Many of these are hollow receptacles that can be filled with small candies or coins by removing the head, upper body, or base of the figure. It is likely that these little presents reflect a continuation of the ancient offering of soul cakes to visitors. Similar but larger favors, up to a foot high, might serve as centerpieces.

Ranging in height from two to six inches, favors are found in many forms, and these highly individualistic objects are among the most charming and popular of Halloween collectibles. The most artistic have usually been molded from plaster of Paris or papier-mâché and hand-painted, although cardboard, paper, cotton, celluloid, and today plastic are also found. Among the most unusual are nodding figures whose heads are attached by wire springs so that they jiggle about when touched.

These wax candles, gruesome in their exact detail, were intended to grace a Halloween table. Even the jolly pumpkin may be carved to resemble a skull. This pair of 8″ high candles bears the label of the Gurley candle-manufacturing company of Buffalo, New York. They were produced c. 1950–60.

Halloween

RIGHT: *The connection of the pumpkin, usually decorated or carved as a face, to Halloween rituals is long-standing but of uncertain origin. The term "jack-o'-lantern" frequently used in describing pumpkin-form lanterns carried by participants in the holiday actually refers to the phosphorescent light produced by rotting vegetation in swampy areas. Long unexplained, these mysterious winking lights were a source of dread to travelers. Since a candle-lit lantern in the hands of a pedestrian creates a similar effect, it would seem that the association was thus established. It is particularly appropriate in the case of this painted sheet-steel jack-o'-lantern, which can be attached to a long pole and carried high above the ground. Nine inches tall, this piece was made in the United States c. 1930–40.*

LEFT: *This painted papier-mâché pumpkin is 9″ tall and was made in Germany c. 1920–30.*

RIGHT: *In European folkways, the jack-o'-lantern represents the soul of one who has been refused admission to both Heaven and Hell, and is doomed to wander the earth until Judgment Day. Understandably annoyed by this, he often leads travelers astray. The unusually graphic rattle is made of lithographed paper and cardboard, 3.5″ in diameter. It is marked* MADE IN GERMANY *and dates to the 1920s.*

LEFT: *More often than not, whatever its sinister antecedents, the jack-o'-lantern is a humorous figure. Here he appears in the guise of a nodding-head toy, or "nodder," decked out in his Sunday best and smoking the cigarette that was both medically and socially acceptable in the 1930s. Marked* MADE IN GERMANY, *the figure is 4″ high and manufactured from plaster of Paris, wire springs, cotton, and lithographed paper.*

BELOW: *While one of these three candy containers is traditional in form, the others are not. In the middle is a witch whose "pumpkin head" is black rather than the usual orange or yellow; the pumpkin at the right supports a mouse, another animal that might be either a witch's familiar or the witch herself, transformed to do greater evil. Ranging in size from 2″ to 3.5″, these examples are made of crepe paper, cardboard, and cotton. They were produced in Germany c. 1910–30.*

The frequent use of the pumpkin form for candy containers may also reflect the vegetable's ancient association with abundance. Among the Chinese it is termed "Emperor of the Garden" and is a symbol of fruitfulness and health, while Parisians once celebrated the Fête du Potiron, or Festival of King Pumpkin, by arraying their largest specimen in crown and tinsel regalia and bearing it about the central market as all paid mock homage. King Pumpkin's fate, however, did not differ from that of his lesser brothers. After the celebration he was cut into pieces which were auctioned off to the crowd. Illustrated here are two small candy container party favors of string, lithographed paper, and cardboard. The valise is marked GERMANY, *and both were made there c. 1925–40. The smaller piece is 2" high, the larger 4".*

Paper table accessories Those who gave children's parties soon realized that candy, cake, and assorted beverages would quickly ruin a linen or cotton tablecloth and napkins. As far back as 1900, manufacturers were providing a variety of paper napkins, plates, cups, and table coverings, as well as crepe-paper streamers and punchout figures of thin cardboard that could be used to embellish the festive board—and other areas of the house. Typically, these items were decorated by the process of lithography, and many make appealing collectibles. However, the use to which they were put assured that few would survive to be collected. Examples dating prior to the 1930s are exceedingly rare.

Some believe that the owl's hoot is a sign of bad luck or death and that even to see an owl may presage misfortune. And, of course, the owl is one of the witch's most trusted familiars. To avoid the bird's evil influence a person may throw salt in the fire, tie a knot in a handkerchief, or even turn his pockets inside out. This group of lanterns ranges in size from 2" to 4.5". All were made in Germany c. 1920–35 of papier-mâché and cardboard with wire handles.

Halloween

LEFT: *Traditional candy containers are in the shape of creatures closely associated with the Halloween tradition—here the cat, the witch, the pumpkin-head figure, and the ghost. The last reflects the ancient belief that on Samain the graves opened and the dead returned to walk the earth. So enduring is this legend that in parts of Italy food is still left on the table for the ghostly visitants. The custom of decorating graves at this time also reflects an attempt to propitiate departed spirits. The candy boxes seen here are 4″ to 5″ high. They are of papier-mâché, crepe paper, and cardboard. The witch is marked* GERMANY, *and all were made there during the 1930s.*

RIGHT: *The appearance of vegetable forms among Halloween novelties may reflect the blending of customs associated with All Hallows Eve and those surrounding Samain, the ancient harvest festival that heralded the beginning of winter and was celebrated on November 1. Feasting and "walking the fields" to ensure their future fertility were traditional at this time. The well-crafted candy containers shown here may be intended to represent gourds or squash. They are of plaster of Paris, 3.5″ to 5″ tall, and made in Germany c. 1920–30. The heads are removable so that candy can be inserted.*

Greeting cards Although the custom has almost totally disappeared today, during the 1920s and 1930s many people exchanged Halloween cards. Printed in the form of lithographed penny postcards, these bore humorous images and sayings. The artwork was frequently done by the most popular illustrators in the field, such as the well-known Frances Brundage. Far less common than Christmas or Valentine's cards, Halloween cards can still be found in sufficient quantity to offer the possibility of an interesting collection.

Lithographed cardboard decorations came in punchout booklets from which they could be removed for table decoration. Some were also sent as Halloween cards. The examples illustrated here, which are 3" high, were published in the United States during the period 1940–60.

Cookie cutters and candy molds Tin cookie cutters in the shape of pumpkins or witch hats were used in preparing holiday sweets, while one can also occasionally encounter the iron, tin, or pot metal molds that manufacturers employed in making Halloween candy. The latter are available in a substantial variety of shapes, including hats, kettles, brooms, cats, various phases of the moon, pumpkins, and the witch on her broomstick. Cookie cutters may date from the late nineteenth century, but most candy molds are of the 1900s.

These two charming lithographed Halloween greeting cards were designed by the popular artist Frances Brundage. They were printed in Germany c. 1920–30.

OPPOSITE: *Party favors displayed on tables for the Halloween meal vary in form. Here we see a pumpkin man, a bottle, a witch's hat, and a kettle whose lid is in the form of a pumpkin face. The hat and the kettle are significant appurtenances of the witch. It was believed that she needed to don the former to work spells, while the kettle or cauldron was the source of both her deadly brews and powers of divination. All are of cardboard, paper, and papier-mâché, 1.5" to 9" high, and were made in Germany c. 1920–40.*

ABOVE: *Simple musical instruments have always played an important role in Halloween festivities, both as a part of the celebration and to ward off by their noise any evil spirits that might be abroad at the time. In seventeenth-century Ireland, groups of horn-blowing country lads visited farmhouses to collect money and food for the traditional Halloween celebration, an early form of trick or treat. Three of the most common noisemakers—a bell, a horn, and a rattle, whose hollow handle serves also as a horn—are shown here. The horn, German made, is of lithographed paper and wood. The other pieces, of lithographed sheet metal and wood, were made in the United States. All date from about 1930–50.*

60

BELOW: *Unlike most other Halloween items noisemakers were frequently manufactured in the United States. Seen here are several rattles or "clackers," horns, a bell, and a drum. All were made of lithographed sheet metal, wood, and paper in the United States or Germany c. 1920–50*

OPPOSITE: *Traditional Halloween figures as well as vegetable forms appear on these tiny stickpins, which were worn with costumes. Only an inch high on the average, these pieces are of plaster of Paris and paper and were produced in Germany c. 1930–40.*

Manufacturers

Better than 75 percent of available Halloween collectibles, including the majority of the most interesting, were made in Germany between 1890 and 1940. Many of these were molded of plaster of Paris, papier-mâché, or composition in small factories or home workshops where their creators were allowed substantial license in painting and decorating. Consequently, many pieces have the look of "one-of-a-kind" folk art rather than a production-line quality. Only a small fraction of these imports are marked, usually GERMANY or MADE IN GERMANY.

After 1930, Japanese firms began to produce similar objects. While they copied the German forms and mode of decoration, the Japanese makers never achieved either the sharpness of detail or the quality of decoration seen in the European work. Again, after World War II, a third line of favors and decorative objects emerged from Hong Kong. Primarily in plastic, these are presently of little interest to collectors though they well may be future collectibles. Examples from both Japan and Hong Kong frequently bear marks of national origin.

Halloween items of American origin are confined primarily to two areas: metalwares and paper goods. Most of the lithographed sheet-tin musical instruments and candle lanterns found were made here. Marx and other well-known toy manufacturers ventured into this field, as did lesser-known metal-stamping works. Even before 1900 American paper doll manufacturers were producing books of Halloween figures that could be punched out and used as table decorations or sent as greeting cards, while most disposable paper tablecloths, napkins, and cups are still made in this country. Patent dates, and the marks USA or MADE IN USA, are frequently seen on these wares.

Thanksgiving

*C*ustoms and objects associated with Thanksgiving reflect the holiday's origin in ancient harvest festivals. Some versions of the tale give an impression that Thanksgiving developed spontaneously from the Plymouth colonists' desire to give thanks for survival in a new and difficult land, and that the settlers introduced this custom to the native Americans; both groups, in fact, were quite familiar with the fall rites.

The Iroquois and other eastern American Indians had established communal dances commemorating the gathering of various fruits and vegetables long before arrival of the whites; and the settlers themselves had as part of their tradition Harvest Home, a day of feasting, dance, and prayer celebrated on the final day of the fall harvest and also called the Ingathering. For both groups, the holiday combined propitiation and thanksgiving to those natural powers that controlled agriculture with a feast upon the fruits of the fields at a time when they were most abundant. The mixture of joy and relief with which the returning pickers were greeted is reflected in the words of the old song "Harvest Home," which was sung as the wagons were unloaded in the farmyard:

OPPOSITE: *One of the rarest forms taken by the festive bird is that of a cast-iron shooting-gallery target. It is, however, a particularly appropriate one, as the turkeys which graced the first American celebration in 1621 were for the most part brought down by the Pilgrims' blunderbusses. This target, which was originally mounted on an iron rod and designed to fall over when hit by shot, is 4.5" high. It was made in the United States c. 1900–30.*

Harvest Home! Harvest Home!
We've plowed, we've sowed
We've reaped, we've mowed
And brought safe home
Every load.

Though the holiday was observed sporadically on these shores from 1621 on, it was in 1789 that George Washington made it official, recommending "to the People of the United States a day of public thanks-giving and prayer to be observed . . . Thursday the 26th day of November. . . ." Washington's declaration dwelt heavily upon the obligation of the nation and its people to respond to God-given freedom

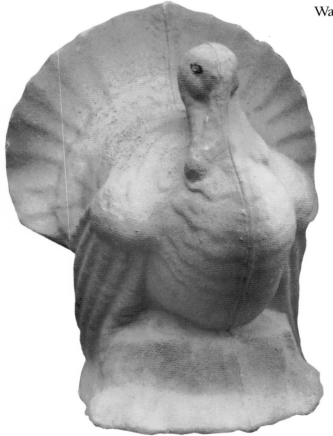

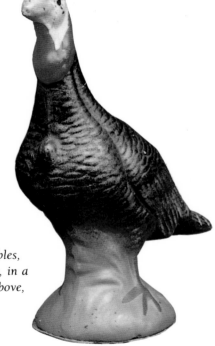

By far the most common of Thanksgiving collectibles, the turkey appears in many guises. Here, at right, in a painted plaster-of-Paris ornament 7″ high, and, above, as a papier-mâché candy container 9″ tall. Both pieces were made in Germany c. 1920–35.

and prosperity by performing "our several and relative duties properly and punctually"; this theme of service has continued as a thread through subsequent Thanksgiving orations.

However, newspaper advertisements make it clear that even in the early 1900s the economic aspects of the event were not overlooked. A florist offered "Flowers for Thanksgiving," a butcher "Thanksgiving Poultry," a hardware store "Thanksgiving cooking utensils"; and even the plumber got into the act, declaring that one should "(g)ive thanks if the plumbing in your house is in perfect order. But if it is old or imperfect have it attended to at once. Poor plumbing enriches the doctors. . . ."

Although earlier Thanksgiving festivities included churchgoing, public speeches and meetings, dances, singing, and general merrymaking as well as the traditional dinner, today, the last is preeminent, and collectibles available are those associated with decoration of the table and dining area. In the nineteenth century, corn shucks, autumn leaves, apples, nuts, gourds, and various fruits were used for this purpose. These still are utilized, particularly the multicolored "Indian corn," which is displayed in bunches on doors—a custom based on the ancient belief in the corn doll or kern baby that was carried home by the harvesters and set up in the barn. Although now the cobs are thought of as a seasonal greeting, in bygone days many believed that the spirit of the Corn Mother or Harvest Mother inhabited the last sheaf and that bringing it home would assure a good crop in the ensuing year.

Today, both door and table are likely to be decorated with commercially manufactured decorations, especially representations of the turkey, which has come to be as closely associated with the holiday as Santa Claus with Christmas or the bunny with Easter.

Types of Thanksgiving Collectibles

Despite the seemingly varied themes—Indians, Pilgrims, fruits, vegetables, meats, and so forth—that might be expected in Thanksgiving-related items, surprisingly little variation is found. By far the most popular and most common symbol is the turkey.

Favors and candy boxes Few Thanksgiving tables are deemed complete without a roast turkey, and the favors, candy boxes, and centerpieces adorning the festive board are generally in the form of turkeys as well. Most sought after are the papier-mâché, plaster-of-Paris, or composition turkeys, both hens and gobblers, which were produced in Germany c. 1910–40. These were usually manufactured in sets consisting of a large gobbler as much as a foot high, and six to twelve smaller companions three to six inches in height.

The finest examples are skillfully molded and hand-painted in naturalistic colors. Eyes may be of glass, and feet and legs are usually of cast lead or heavy wire. The head is removable or the body can be separated in the middle to allow for the insertion of candy.

Less often seen are similarly constructed chickens, particularly roosters, as well as ducks, and even pigeons. Their seeming lack of popularity in this country reflects our customs. Duck or goose is a Christmas dish; chicken was eaten on the great holiday only by those who could not obtain turkey; and who would grace their Thanksgiving table with a pigeon?

Other favors and candy containers (often the same figure would be made both as a favor and a candy box, the former being solid) include figures of Pilgrim men and maids complete with top hats and blunderbuss guns.

In pursuit of realism, some manufacturers turned out turkey favors that were made of dyed cotton wound on a wire matrix and then adorned with feathers, both dyed and natural. Their flexible thin wire feet allowed these pieces to be attached to wall lamps, curtain rods, and other surfaces.

Paper table accessories For the convenience of those who prepared and served the lavish holiday meal, manufacturers produced from the late 1800s on such disposable items as napkins, table coverings, plates, cups, and assorted decorations. These were lithographed in bright colors and usually featured the day's bill of fare. Most sought after among these are the embossed, litho-graphed, cardboard turkeys, often as much as 14″ tall, which served as table and mantel decorations. These sometimes have a flaring crepe-paper tail or base.

Greeting cards Though not as popular as during the 1920s and 1930s, the custom of giving Thanksgiving greeting cards continues. The earlier cards were largely German made, of the penny-postal variety. Since the 1950s, however, most people have chosen to send cards in envelopes. The great majority of these are American, made by Hallmark and other well-known manufacturers. While sometimes charming, Thanksgiving cards have never achieved the artistic level of those sent at Christmas or on Valentine's Day.

LEFT: *A candy container in the form of a turkey, or more rarely a goose or pigeon, was placed before each diner at the table. This example is of painted papier-mâché with cast-lead legs and feet and glass eyes. The head may be removed for access to the storage area. The bird is 8″ high. Similar pieces range in size from 5″ to 12″. All were made in Germany c. 1910–30.*

RIGHT: *Though the Thanksgiving Day table is seldom decorated today, it was often the custom during the 1930s and 1940s to embellish the dining room with various representations of the national bird. This 14″-high lithographed cardboard turkey could stand on the table or mantel or be hung in a window. It was made in the United States c. 1940–50.*

Toys There are few true toys associated with Thanksgiving, probably because gift giving is not a regular part of the holiday ceremony. Shown here, though, is a cotton, fabric, and feather "Tucky" turkey that was manufactured by Steiff of Germany c. 1950–70. There is also at least one board game which deals with the plight of a turkey attempting to avoid his Thanksgiving Day fate!

Miscellaneous items For those who preferred their turkeys on the wing, Victorian communities provided live turkey shoots at which, for a fee, men might shoot at domestic birds released before their guns. At a time when wild turkeys had largely vanished (not the case today, when the wily gobbler thrives in various states), this no doubt provided some with a chance to relive the Pilgrim experience. When this cruel practice was outlawed in the early 1900s, marksmen turned to shooting galleries where they fired at cast-iron targets in the same form. Mounted on horizontal steel rods, these three- to six-inch birds would flip over when struck. Though not easily found, such targets are popular with collectors.

Even in the late nineteenth century the artificial was often substituted for the real. Thanksgiving tables might be embellished not with fresh fruits but with ones carved from marble and then carefully tinted to resemble the genuine article. Extremely attractive and found in great variety, marble fruit is once again gracing the holiday tables of many Americans.

Manufacturers

The majority of the older Thanksgiving favors and candy boxes were produced in German factories and workers' homes during the early years of this century. They are sometimes marked GERMANY or MADE IN GERMANY, though more often this information appeared on the boxes (now usually lost) in which they came. During the 1940s and 1950s several manufacturers in the United States turned out similar though less high-quality items, usually turkeys made from a coarse cardboard-like material sometimes referred to among collectors as "egg-crate" composition. These birds were generally given an overall tan or reddish-brown stain and lacked the details of imported pieces.

The Japanese were also active in this market, copying the German candy containers during the 1930s. Their work, which is rarely identified, is more brightly painted and roughly detailed. During the same period Japanese manufacturers offered celluloid turkeys as table favors, their fanned tails serving to hold a place card.

Other nations joined the Thanksgiving parade. Stone fruit were hand-cut and -painted in Italy during the late nineteenth and early twentieth centuries. They are now being reproduced. Metal collectibles such as shooting-gallery targets are of American manufacture, and often bear a U.S. patent number or date; while paper ephemera such as napkins and cups were made almost exclusively in this country, especially after World War II. The same was true of greeting cards, which were previously made primarily in Germany.

In pursuit of realism, feathers, both dyed and in a natural state, were combined with shaped cotton bodies to produce facsimile turkeys. On the opposite page is a "Tucky" made in Germany, c. 1950–70, by Steiff, the well-known firm of toymakers; it is 4″ high. The other two turkeys above, each 3.5″ tall, were also produced in that country, but around 1930–40. All have iron-wire legs and glass eyes.

71

Christmas

By far the most popular and widely celebrated of holidays, in this country and the entire Western world, is Christmas. And, appropriately enough, it is this event that has spawned the greatest variety of holiday memorabilia.

The Christian festival of the Nativity, Christ's birth, was initially celebrated on various days in December, January, or March (in Armenia it is still observed on January 6); but in the fifth century it was fixed on December 25, a date that coincided with the close of the Roman observances of the Saturnalia (a pagan festival marked by singing, dancing, drinking, and general license) and the Mithric holiday marking the "birth" of the sun.

This choice was a calculated one, for it tended to focus the exuberance and devotional frenzy that had characterized the pagan rituals on the new holiday. However, the coincidence of dates was not without its problems. Ancient customs clung to the new. Throughout the Middle Ages the Christmastide revels, generally covering the twelve days from Christmas to Epiphany and presided over by a popularly elected and aptly named "Lord of Misrule," were marked by the most wanton behavior; so much so that in 1644 the English Parliament attempted to forbid the annual celebration.

Moreover, certain elements of the pre-Christian observances became part of the religious holiday. The great yule log, a bit of which was burned on each of

OPPOSITE: *Although the American tradition of having someone dress up as Santa Claus and distribute gifts dates from the nineteenth century, few early costumes have survived. This mask of painted, sized-cotton gauze dates to the early 1900s. Some 10" in height, the mask was bound about the head with cotton bands, a precursor of the more familiar elastic.*

Known in Germany as Kriss Kringle, in France as Le Père Noël, and in England as Father Christmas, Santa Claus has evolved in the past century from a thin, aesthetic figure to the current symbol of conspicuous consumption. Typical of the earlier form is this 16"-high mantel decoration of felt and cotton netting over a wire matrix. The face and hands are of composition and the beard of rabbit fur. Made in Germany around 1900, the figure carries a tree of dyed goose feathers.

the twelve days of Christmas, was believed to protect the home from fire and lightning, ensure a wealth of crops, and cause cows to bear their young without problems. Mistletoe, sacred to the ancient Celtic Druids, was hung above the doorway not only to encourage romance but also because it was thought to protect against poisons and heal all wounds.

Many other pagan beliefs are associated with the Christian traditions: that a white Christmas presages a prosperous year, a hot or cloudy one death and misfortune; that a person born on Christmas Day can see spirits; and that good luck will come from eating cake prepared for the holiday: ". . . for every Yuletide cake and every cheese tasted at a neighbor's house, a happy month will be added to one's life. . . ." Even today in Louisiana some keep berries from the Christmas holly for good luck or believe that a leaf hung where cattle can see it on Christmas Eve will assure the animals' health during the coming year.

By far the most important secular folklore relating to Christmas is that concerning St. Nicholas, or Santa Claus. Patron saint of Russia, thieves, sailors, virgins, and, of course, children, St. Nicholas was born in Lycia, Asia Minor, around A.D. 352. At an early age he distinguished himself by his good deeds, giving all he had to the poor, and when that was gone miraculously procuring more to distribute in the same manner.

In the American colonies children followed Dutch customs in putting their shoes outside the door on the eve of St. Nicholas's feast day, December 6. If they had been good in the previous year, presents would be found the following day. Bad behavior was "rewarded" with a bundle of switches. The saint's traditional symbol, three bags of gold (marking his generosity), has over the years become the well-known bulging sack of presents.

There was, however, another gift-giving tradition. On Christmas Eve in Germany as far back as the sixteenth century a man of each village, dressed in high

Unlike the present traditional costume of red and white, the turn-of-the-century Santa Claus was often clothed in a variety of colors. These painted plaster-of-Paris and papier-mâché figures are in red, yellow, brown, and blue (they may also be found in green, white, purple, pink, and black). Those illustrated were made in Germany c. 1900–10 and range in height from 5″ to 8″.

boots, white robe, blond wig, and mask, would knock at every door to inquire of parents as to the behavior of their children. Upon receiving favorable answers, he would pass out toys that had previously been brought to him by the adults. Bad children would get the usual bundle of switches.

This gift giver was called Knecht Ruprecht, or "Knight Rupert," and he identified himself as the servant of the Christ Child, who was seen as the ultimate benefactor. In time these traditions merged, with an impersonator of St. Nicholas questioning the children on December 6 as to their desires (the origin of our own department-store Santas), and presents then being distributed on Christmas Eve, allegedly by Kriss Kringle ("Little Christ Child") but actually by the family.

The reindeer-drawn sleigh is an American tradition, apparently originating with Clement Clarke Moore's epic poem *A Visit from St. Nicholas*, published in 1823 (the Dutch St. Nicholas rode a horse). Santa's elves replaced Knecht Ruprecht (known in this country as Black Pete); and a variety of earlier costumes ("Sinti Klass" in 1848 Albany, New York, sounded much more like Rip Van Winkle, being described as wearing a three-cornered hat and silver-buckled shoes and smoking a long clay pipe!) gave way to the familiar red and white garb. During the twentieth century, the traditional depiction of Santa Claus as a thin, aesthetic, almost emaciated, individual was replaced by the familiar roly-poly gourmand with whom we are familiar.

Crimped and cut-paper roping was wrapped over a cardboard matrix to produce these inexpensive but appealing tree or window decorations. The boot with paper wrappings is a candy container. The wreath has a velvet bow and artificial sprigs of pine, while the star is embellished with a silver-foil insert. All were made in Germany c. 1920–40. Height 4–9".

The decorated Christmas tree originated in Germany, where as early as 1605 a *Weihnachtsbaum,* or "Holy Night Tree," was set up in the public square at Strasbourg. During the past century or so this tradition has spread to other countries, including our own. Although most such trees were and are decorated with tinsel, lights, bulbs, and other ornaments (all now grist for the collector's mill), in the early twentieth century they might be festooned with gifts to be given to the poor.

Types of Christmas Collectibles

Objects associated with the celebration of Christmas are not only the most abundant of all holiday memorabilia; they were also the first to come to the attention of collectors. As far back as the 1940s there were enthusiasts in the field, and today they are legion. In part this is due to the importance of the day; more critical, though, is the diversity and quantity available.

Collectors may focus on Santa Claus figures, variations of which run into the hundreds; the thousands of different tree decorations; lights, both electric and candle-powered; ephemera, including greeting cards and paper used in decoration and table settings; candy boxes and other favors; costumes and masks and Christmas-related toys. There is even some folk art.

Santa Claus figures Historically, the Christ Child was the focus of the Christmas ritual, but his place has been largely usurped by the secularized Santa Claus, who has even appropriated the title Kriss Kringle or "Little Christ Child." A collection of Santa figures could easily run into the hundreds and include objects serving a variety of purposes from table decorations through toys to folk art.

By far the most common, though, are papier-mâché, plaster-of-Paris, composition, wood, plastic, cotton, or cloth table and mantel decorations. These range in height from 3″ to 18″, and in quality from mediocre molded celluloid to handcrafted papier-mâché and plaster of Paris with features and details that are almost sculptural in quality.

Late-nineteenth- and early-twentieth-century examples, made primarily in Germany, are lean to the point of gauntness. Santa's hands are often drawn within the sleeves of his voluminous medieval robes as though seeking to escape the cold, and in place of the expected bag of gifts he clutches a

OPPOSITE: *Though frequently seen in wreaths and other decorations, paper roping is seldom utilized in Santa Claus costumes. These three rare examples, ranging in height from 7" to 10", were intended as table or mantel decorations. Their molded plaster-of-Paris faces are very well done, and each bears a different Christmas symbol—the shepherd's staff, the feather tree, and the holly. German, c. 1910–20.*

ABOVE: *Early Santa Claus figures were often as finely molded as dolls of the same period. This c. 1880–1900 example has porcelain-bisque arms and legs and a sensitively formed composition head. The crocheted cotton cap and medieval-looking burlap gown bear little resemblance to the present costume. Of German manufacture, this piece is 8" tall.*

RIGHT: *In this detail of one of the Santas on the opposite page, one can see the work lavished on the plaster-of-Paris face. The hand-painted mask, in the form of a disc, was glued with the cotton-batting beard to the crimped-paper body.*

Christmas tree of dyed feathers, a bunch of holly, a shepherd's crook (reflecting an attempt to recover those who have gone astray), or even a basket of woven splint. Nor is his costume immediately recognizable, for rather than the usual red trimmed in white, it may be white, yellow, brown, pink, green, purple, or even black.

His beard can be of rabbit fur or cotton batting, and in the better examples his features are carefully hand-painted to create a most lifelike expression, though one that is often fierce, sometimes almost crazed, and hardly ever like the jolly, simple-minded look to which we have now become accustomed.

There can be no doubt that these bizarre, emaciated figures reflect the nineteenth-century vision of Santa Claus, for they appear also in contemporary magazines. A Santa illustrated in the December 28, 1872, issue of *Punch* looks like a Bowery bum, with unkempt hair, ragged robes, and worn-out shoes; and a predecessor seen in *The Great Pictorial Annual Brother Jonathan* for January 1, 1845, is so slim that he might slide unscathed down the narrowest of chimneys.

Santas of the 1930–60 period, on the other hand, have taken on a reassuringly rotund profile, reflecting the efforts of the great American cartoonist Thomas Nast, who as early as 1879 was depicting the jolly old elf in *Harper's Weekly* as a lovable butterball.

Either type served as table, mantel, and under-tree decorations, and many were also candy containers. In the latter instance, the head might be removable; or, more often, the base could be pulled out and sugar candies poured into the hollow body.

There were also porcelain Santas, either bisque or glazed, as well as those made, primarily in the United States, of pressed or "egg-crate" cardboard. The latter, like the celluloid examples produced in Germany, Japan, and the United States between 1920 and 1950, are seldom very artistic. On the other hand, they are common and much less expensive than earlier papier-mâché and plaster-of-Paris pieces.

Santa Claus masks and costumes

The custom of gift giving by a man or woman clad to resemble the Santa Claus figure seems to have had its origin in sixteenth-century Germany; however, it was not until some three hundred years later that the costume which we recognize evolved.

Masks are generally of papier-mâché or stiffened cloth, sometimes embellished with cotton beards. Better examples are elaborately hand-painted and resemble the more common Halloween masks, which were often made in the same German shops. The best suits are of silk, wool, or velvet, with real leather belts. Most, though, are of cotton velveteen, with boots and belts made from oilcloth. They were produced in Germany, Japan, and the United States.

Favors and candy boxes Although the majority of favors and candy containers are in the form of Santa Claus, other items may also be found. Most popular are snowmen, usually of papier-mâché and separating at the head or middle; reindeer, which may be of composition covered with felt "fur"; and children dressed to play in the snow, with bisque faces and hands and even cardboard churches.

Certain cardboard and paper Christmas tree decorations also are designed as candy containers so that children may find sustenance as well as beauty on the family fir. Christmas stockings and cornucopia are most often seen, but among the odder (and rarer) specimens are round lithographed paper containers featuring the Man in the Moon.

RIGHT: *Painted papier-mâché candy containers in the form of snowmen remain relatively common. This one is 6″ tall and was made in Germany c. 1920–40. It was probably designed as a party favor with small sugar candies inserted through a hole in the base, which was covered with a stamped-tin lid.*

OPPOSITE: *More complex than most party favors, this candy container features a Santa Claus with cotton body covered by a net vest with tiny blown-glass buttons and cotton-felt sleeves. His face is of celluloid, and he has a cotton string about his neck. The automobile is of cardboard with wooden rod axles. Manufactured in Germany c. 1925–35, the piece is 7″ long.*

ABOVE: *The holiday season traditionally is one of parties and dinners, and such paper collectibles as napkins, plates, and cups may be found. This lithographed 12″ fluted-cardboard plate features the Christmas angel surrounded by people involved in a variety of Yuletide activities. Made in Germany, the plate dates from the 1950s.*

OPPOSITE: *More traditional favors are the figures shown here. The Santa in red is a candy box with removable legs; he has papier-mâché face, feet, and hands, a rabbit-fur beard, and cotton-flannel coat. While the feather tree he carries is customary, his handwoven splint basket is rare. His companion is dressed in a flannel coat over cardboard body and also has papier-mâché hands, face, and feet, with cotton beard. Over his shoulder he bears a crepe-paper bag. Ten and 12″ in height, the figures were made in Germany c. 1920–30.*

Mantel decorations There are a surprisingly large number of mantel or center table decorations with a Christmas theme. The standard topic is Santa Claus in his reindeer-drawn sleigh, the open box of which may be filled with greenery, small gift-wrapped packages, or candy. An interesting variation, produced in Japan during the 1950s, features a somewhat perplexed Santa urging on a pair of celluloid reindeer who are drawing a large birch yule log that has been drilled to serve as a candleholder.

Mantel decorations range in length from 12″ to 22″ and are generally rather late, dating after 1940. They also served to embellish the base of the family tree.

Christmas tree decorations Legend has it that Hessian soldiers introduced the decorated Christmas tree into Pennsylvania during Revolutionary War times. There is no doubt that the tradition, probably based on ancient pagan celebrations of the winter solstice, may be traced to Germany where, in the early 1800s, families would decorate a Christmas pyramid consisting of several round flat platforms graded in size from top to bottom and mounted on a central shaft. This treelike device was covered with cut evergreens, and decorations and candles were placed on the shelves. Such pyramids are extremely rare today.

RIGHT: *At 10″ in height, this painted plaster-of-Paris Santa Claus is not the largest of his kind—similar ornaments as much as 24″ tall are known. The feather tree is a traditional feature of such figures. Made in Germany c. 1900–20.*

LEFT: *Although never as popular with buyers or collectors as other materials, celluloid proved an inexpensive material widely used during the pre–World War II period. This 7″-high, molded-celluloid Santa was made in Japan c. 1930–50.*

At their best, Christmas decorations can approach the quality of folk art. This German Santa mounted on horseback combines artistic sensitivity with fine craftsmanship in a large figure that was probably intended to be placed under the Christmas tree or on a mantel. Standing 10″ high by 12″ long, it was made c. 1920–30. The reindeer is of cotton felt over a carved wooden body, with metal horns, and leather and tin harness. Santa has papier-mâché face, hands, and boots, a cloth body, and cotton beard. He carries a feather tree with brass bell.

ABOVE: *A Japanese-made reindeer-drawn sleigh designed as a mantel ornament or centerpiece. Marked* MADE IN JAPAN, *it was produced c. 1930–60. The deer are of celluloid, the sleigh is made of painted wood, and Santa has papier-mâché head and hands, a cotton-felt coat, and rabbit-fur beard. The piece is 19″ long.*

BELOW: *These celluloid reindeer are bearing a birch yule log, drilled to serve as a candleholder for the mantel. Traditionally, the yule log is burned a bit on each of the twelve days of the holiday season, and in some countries a portion of it is saved to kindle the next year's log. In France and parts of Scandinavia it is thought that this preserved fragment will protect the house from lightning. Sixteen inches long, this ornament was made in Japan c. 1950–60. The Santa is of papier-mâché and cotton flannel, with a cotton beard; the chain is brass.*

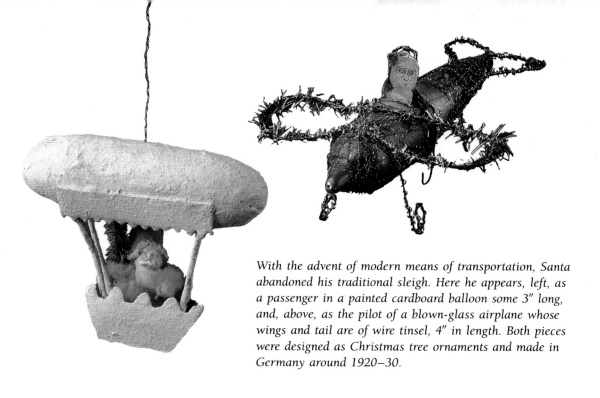

With the advent of modern means of transportation, Santa abandoned his traditional sleigh. Here he appears, left, as a passenger in a painted cardboard balloon some 3″ long, and, above, as the pilot of a blown-glass airplane whose wings and tail are of wire tinsel, 4″ in length. Both pieces were designed as Christmas tree ornaments and made in Germany around 1920–30.

One reason for use of the pyramid rather than a live tree may have been the weight of the first decorations. Known as Kugels, or Kuglen, these were of blown glass lined with zinc or lead and sometimes covered with colored wax. They came in three shapes, ball, pear, and bunch of grapes, and ranged in size up to 14″. Since the glass was sometimes a quarter-inch thick, larger ornaments were far too heavy to be supported by a branch. In fact, many were hung from the ceiling.

Kuglen were made as early as 1820, and a surprising number have survived to grace contemporary collections. Most are silver, gold, cobalt blue, or green. Examples in red or amethyst are prized as rarities.

A major breakthrough in decorative technology occurred in 1860, when Louis Greiner-Schlotfeger of Lauscha in the

RIGHT:*This cotton-batting Christmas tree ornament is in the form of a snowman, who wears a cardboard stovepipe hat and carries a bunch of twigs. While he bears a resemblance to Charlie Chaplin, the figure is probably Knecht Ruprecht (literally, Knight Rupert), the North German Christmas figure who gave presents or rods for punishment depending upon whether a child had been good or bad during the year. Four inches high and dated c. 1920–30, this piece is German in origin.*

The first thin-walled Christmas bulbs were blown in Lauscha, Germany, by Louis Greiner-Schlotfeger, in about 1860; and from then until World War II, German makers dominated the market. These hand-painted Santa Claus figures vary in size from 3" to 4.5" and are typical of the period 1920–35.

Thuringian Forest of Germany introduced a new type of ornament at the Sonneberg toy market. These too were of glass, but paper thin, light in weight, and blown in a variety of forms—balls, apples, icicles, pinecones, acorns, nuts, mushrooms, berries, peaches, pears, and even bananas. The interior of each piece was coated with silver nitrate for reflection and the exterior lacquered in one or more colors.

Greiner's innovation swept the country, and by the 1880s factories in the Lauscha region as well as others in Bohemia were turning out millions of bulbs yearly in a thousand different patterns. These fragile decorations are now pursued by a growing collecting fraternity.

Blown-glass ornaments have been manufactured from the 1860s to the present time; however, their greatest period of production was c. 1880–1940. Most examples fall into one of several broad categories. There are human and fanciful figures, including men and women (both heads and full-size figures), angels, cartoon characters, clowns; such odd choices as the Devil and the Man in the Moon; and, of course, Santa Claus.

Animals and birds are plentiful. Among the former are cats and dogs, pigs, squirrels, horses, and even fish and frogs, while the latter encompass peacocks, chickens, owls, parrots, and turkeys. There are also many vehicles—autos, airplanes, ships, balloons, dirigibles—as well as a variety of fruits and such miscellaneous objects as musical instruments (including horns that can be blown), baseballs, and even pistols.

The advent of these lighter glass bulbs spurred the use of indoor trees, not only natural ones but also artificial "feather trees" composed of wooden dowel trunks, their branches embellished with dyed turkey or goose feathers. Most feather trees are small, though a few in the five- to six-foot range are encountered.

And, of course, not all collectible ornaments are of glass. A few

LEFT: *Not all Christmas bulbs were in the form of Santas or even related in form to the season. The two gourdlike ornaments seen here reflect the whimsy so often found in German glass blowers, who produced over 5,000 known variations. The gourd head is 3" high, while the man is 5". His velour arms and legs are unusual. Both are German, c. 1920–40.*

RIGHT: *Hand-blown German Christmas tree ornaments from the 1920s. The horn actually makes a sound, while the teardrop-shaped bulb contains a lithographed cardboard or "scrap" angel.*

Cotton was a popular material for tree decorations. These three Santa Claus figures are of cotton batting and paper, with lithographed die-cut features. The small Santa beating a drum is quite unusual. Ranging in height from 3.5" to 6", all were made in Germany, c. 1915–25.

These lithographed, embossed cardboard and artificial angel-hair ornaments are in the form of St. Nicholas, patron saint of Russia and the prototype from which the American Santa Claus figure developed. Born in the fourth century A.D., St. Nicholas spent his life giving gifts to the poor. The medieval symbol of three bags of gold associated with the saint evolved into the bag of toys borne by the present-day Santa. The Russian cap rather than the usual hood reflects his origin. Made in Germany for export to eastern Europe, c. 1900–20.

These lithographed paper and tinsel ornaments include a pair of cones in which candy canes or other sweets could be placed. The highly sophisticated die-cut lithography is comparable to that found in children's books of the same period. The cones are 7.5" long, and the bell is 5" high. All are of German manufacture and date to the 1920s.

were made of wax or wax over composition. Though remarkably lifelike, these were also fragile; examples in good condition are hard to come by. Much easier to acquire are ornaments of rolled and shaped cotton batting. These were painted, clothed in crepe paper or even silk, and in the case of the many human figures, given faces of die-cut, lithographed paper. Many different animals can be found in cotton.

The so-called Dresden ornaments form another broad category. These were made of stamped cardboard, and were generally covered with gold or silver foil. They are remarkably detailed and appear in a variety unmatched in other decorations. Highly realistic human figures, animals, vehicles, and even household items such as clocks, purses, and shoes may be found. Made around 1900, Dresdens were popular in Europe but not in the United States, where relatively few occur.

There are also paper ornaments. Most common are the lithographed paper-over-cardboard balls that open to form a candy box, and the wreaths, stars, and Christmas stockings made of crimped and cut-paper roping. These might be hung on a tree or used as door or window decoration. Lithographed die-cut paper was also often combined with cloth, spun glass, tinsel, or cotton webbing to create frail and fanciful ornaments that clung like moths to the family tree.

Finally, since the end of World War II plastic ornaments have become more and more a part of the Christmas scene. Most were made in Japan or the United States and designed to resemble blown-glass bulbs. Collector interest in the earlier and more artistic examples is increasing; if one wishes to collect inexpensively, now is the time.

Christmas lights The first tree lights were candles that were secured in tiny tin holders clamped to the branches, a method also employed with some early glass ornaments. The obvious dangers involved led to the introduction of tin and glass candle lanterns and cuplike holders of blown or pressed glass. These latter were of colored glass (red, blue, amber, and green were popular), and held a small wick that floated in oil atop water. Hanging from the branches by wire loops, they added a particularly festive air to the Christmas scene. Such "tumbler lights" can still be found and are highly collectible.

The search for something safer continued, though, and on November 23, 1901, the General Electric Company of Schenectady, New York, advertised in *Scientific American* strings of miniature carbon lights—the first electric Christmas bulbs. Initially, these were nothing more than tiny, tinted light bulbs, but by 1910, figural examples—fruits, nuts, and flowers—appeared.

LEFT: *Cloth ornaments had the advantage that they were unbreakable. This lithographed Santa is stuffed with cotton batting and is 3″ high. During the late nineteenth and early twentieth centuries, dolls were often made in the same manner. This one is American, c. 1910–20.*

ABOVE: *Basket-form Christmas tree decorations such as these are so fragile that few have survived. Made in Germany c. 1910–25, they are composed of celluloid hands and faces, with cloth clothing glued to cotton mesh which in turn is secured to a woven twig basket in one case and one made of paper rope over cardboard in the other. The pieces are 2.5″ and 3.5″ high, respectively.*

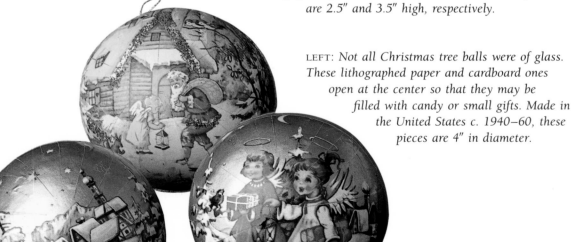

LEFT: *Not all Christmas tree balls were of glass. These lithographed paper and cardboard ones open at the center so that they may be filled with candy or small gifts. Made in the United States c. 1940–60, these pieces are 4″ in diameter.*

These were the forerunners of the thousands of different figural light bulbs now available to collectors.

Interestingly enough, some early commentators doubted that the public would embrace the new fad. A writer for the December 1926 issue of *Good Housekeeping* magazine argued that while "bulbs blown in shapes of fruit, animals, figures, etc., are interesting and attractive [they] do not have the lasting qualities of conventional conical shapes. . . ." Either performance was not a consideration for most, or technical improvements extended the lives of figural bulbs, for these have been made and used in vast quantities.

In design, figural lights generally follow Christmas tree bulbs. In fact, in some cases the same mold was used to blow both the decoration and the light. Human figures (including the so-called character bulbs, featuring current comic-strip characters such as Betty Boop, Little Orphan Annie, and Popeye) and animals are most often seen. But there are also vehicles, fruits, and vegetables, and even such unexpected objects as ice-cream cones and hamburgers complete with onion and bun!

Since many of these lights are thirty to sixty years old, most no longer work. This is not regarded as a disability by the typical collector, who acquires them for their form rather than their function.

Although most Christmas tree lights are two inches or less in length, a few larger examples were made during the 1920s, and these are highly prized by collectors. Most often found is Santa Claus, ranging from four to ten inches in height.

Wax candles for use at the table, in windows, or on the mantel are of considerable antiquity. Sixteenth-century German homes showed a single candle at the window to light the way of Kriss Kringle. However, figural candles are

Although the first successful Christmas tree lights were marketed by the General Electric Company in 1901, the so-called character bulbs, those in the form of people, animals, vehicles, and the like, did not appear in quantity until the 1920s. Among the most popular were oversize Santas such as this 10″-example, which was produced in Japan c. 1920–30 and bears the mark of a Japanese firm, Eagle. Large lights of this sort were designed for use in window or shop displays rather than for the tree.

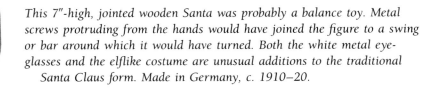

This 7"-high, jointed wooden Santa was probably a balance toy. Metal screws protruding from the hands would have joined the figure to a swing or bar around which it would have turned. Both the white metal eyeglasses and the elflike costume are unusual additions to the traditional Santa Claus form. Made in Germany, c. 1910–20.

a recent innovation. Few can be found that date prior to the 1930s. The mostpopular designs are Santa, snowballs and snowmen, angels, and candy canes.

Christmas toys Appropriately enough, almost all toys with a Christmas theme feature St. Nick himself. There are push-and-pull toys such as the wood and lithographed paper Santa, sleigh, and reindeer produced by R. Bliss of Pawtucket, Rhode Island, in the 1890s, and the cast-iron version of the same theme made by the Hubley Manufacturing Company at Lancaster, Pennsylvania, around 1920. There are jointed figures of Santa Claus and a surprising variety of wood and celluloid jack-in-the-boxes. Also found are mechanical toys such as a walking Santa Claus and a rocking-horse Santa mounted on a reindeer. To encourage thrift, there is even a Santa Claus mechanical bank. A coin is placed in his upraised hand, a lever depressed, and the cash deposited in a chimney-like bank.

Moreover, there are enough books, paper dolls, puzzles, and games developing the Christmas theme to allow for a specialized collection of these alone. In 1900 one firm, Parker Brothers of Salem, Massachusetts, was advertising no less than five different Christmas-oriented board games: "Christmas Dinner," "Kriss Kringle," "Merry Christmas," "Night Before Christmas," and "Santa Claus."

Greeting cards The first Christmas card was designed in 1843 at the behest of Henry Cole, a London business-man. Divided into three panels, the most important of which showed family members joining in a Yuletide toast, it bore the now-familiar greeting: "A Merry Christmas and a Happy New Year to You."

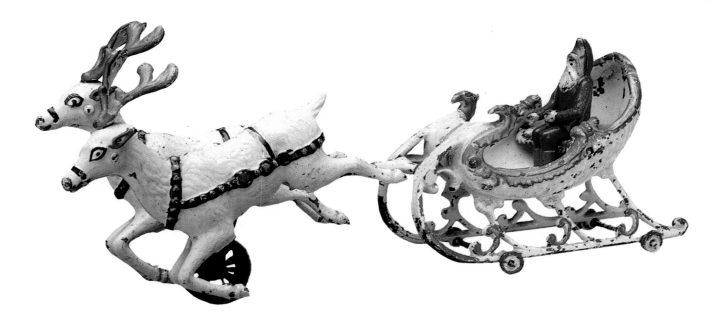

ABOVE: *Toys with a Christmas theme are less common than decorations; however, a substantial number exist. This painted, cast-iron sleigh drawn by reindeer was made by the Hubley Manufacturing Company of Lancaster, Pennsylvania, c. 1921. It is 13" long. The wheels beneath the deer are so balanced that when the toy is pushed or pulled along, the animals seem to gallop.*

LEFT: *Another American-made Christmas toy, this lithographed paper and wood sleigh is 18" long. It bears the printed label of the R. Bliss Manufacturing Company of Pawtucket, Rhode Island, and was produced around 1890. The interior of the sleigh could be filled with candy or evergreens and the piece used as a centerpiece or mantel decoration.*

A
MERRY CHRISTMAS

Only a dozen examples of this card are known, but the many collectors of Christmas missives have available to them literally thousands of other examples. Some of these, including the most elaborate mechanical and three-dimensional, are envelope cards. Many others are penny postals. The Hallmark Historical Collection, owned by Hallmark Cards of Kansas City, Missouri, houses over forty thousand of both.

Greeting-card manufacturers were active in England and France by the 1860s, but the first major American producer was Louis Prang of Boston, who printed his first Christmas card in 1875, and by 1881 was turning out five million cards a year, most of them for the Yuletide season. Prang cards are today among the most sought after, rivaled only by those bearing the name of the important designer Kate Greenaway.

Around the turn of the century Germany entered the lists with inexpensive penny postals, a form of greeting that remained popular into the 1930s. To the surprise of the novice collector, many of these early examples bear little resemblance to contemporary Christmas cards. Rather than Santa Claus or a snowy scene, they may feature a bouquet of flowers symbolizing longing for spring and the hope embodied in the birth of Christ. Only the greeting reveals their purpose.

Most collectors focus on pre–World War II Christmas cards; however, some interesting later examples exist. These, particularly the mechanical or "pop-up" ones, will certainly attain collectible status.

Folk art Quite a few folk artists have turned their attention to the Christmas hol-

RIGHT: *Another unusual application of the Santa Claus motif is seen in this tissue-paper and painted papier-mâché candle lantern. Extremely well detailed, it is 9″ high, dates from 1910–30, and was produced in a German shop. Lanterns such as this were carried by the groups of carolers who went from house to house during the festive season.*

OPPOSITE: *This c. 1900–10 German postcard shows Santa Claus as he was first depicted—a thin, almost aesthetic-looking wanderer.*

iday. Perhaps the earliest and certainly the most widespread craft is that of creche manufacture. Carvers from Italy to Mexico have, over the past four hundred years, created many versions of the manger, the Wise Men, the Christ Child, his adoring parents, and the various animals said to have been present. Age, quality of carving, and painted surface are the things looked for by collectors.

At a later date, in the mid-nineteenth century, large numbers of chalkware figures were manufactured, usually in Italy, for sale in the United States. The Germanic settlers of Pennsylvania were particularly fond of these colorful painted mantel decorations. Among examples associated with the Christmas season are large churches (very rare), reindeer and lambs, and Santa Claus figures.

Santa was also the subject of one of America's greatest folk carvers. Samuel A. Robb of New York City (1851–1928), a well-known sculptor of ship's figureheads and tobacconist's figures, carved at least two rotund Santas around 1880. Both were about three feet high, and one was carved as a Yuletide gift for a young relative.

Manufacturers

It was in Germany that the first glass tree decorations were produced, and the finest papier-mâché and plaster-of-Paris Santa Claus or Father Christmas figures were made there too, primarily between 1880 and 1935. Many of these pieces bear the familiar mark GERMANY or MADE IN GERMANY.

German manufacturers also turned out most of the decorations in cotton batting, bisque, and composition. However, during the 1920s and 1930s Japanese companies provided stiff competition, and from 1920 to 1940 Japan dominated the celluloid field. In all areas Japanese examples can be distinguished by their lack of detail and unusually pink flesh tones.

American manufacturers were prominent in the manufacture of celluloid and cardboard decorations and, until challenged by the Japanese after 1915, controlled the Christmas tree lighting market. Domestic concerns also made

OPPOSITE: *Though seldom as elaborate as those given on Valentine's Day, Christmas cards can be charming. More than seven million are now mailed each year, yet few could compare with this lithographed cardboard and crepe-paper example which dates to the 1920s. Made in the United States, it bears a patent date of July 14, 1925.*

Jingle,
jingle,
Here's old Santa
With his toys
and pretty
tree
And he's bringing
all good wish
Straight to
you from me

PATENTED
July 14, 1926.

most of the glass candy containers and a substantial number of the games and toys associated with the holiday.

The first American Christmas tree ornaments were turned out in 1871 by William DeMuth of New York City, who advertised his product as "silvered glass balls in a variety of colors and strings of glass beads for the decoration of the Christmas tree. . . ." It was not until the mid-1930s, though, that well-established domestic competition for the foreign imports emerged. First in the field was the Premier Glass Works of New Jersey. By the early 1940s its competitors included the Paragon Glass Works of Lewiston, Maine, and the well-known Corning Glass Works, located in the New York State community of the same name. While of interest to some collectors, the American products have not captured the general imagination in the way the German and even the Japanese products have.

PATRIOTIC
HOLIDAYS

*T*oday, it is really only the Fourth of July that is nationally celebrated, but not so many years ago both elaborate public display and general private observation in the United States centered on numerous national dates, including presidential birthdays, Columbus Day, Memorial Day, and even local events such as Boston's Patriots' Day and various southern commemorations focused on the rise and fall of the Confederacy. Some of these, particularly Independence Day, have generated a substantial quantity of memorabilia—objects such as table decorations and favors designed to be used in conjunction with celebratory meals, as well as toys, folk art, and costumes made to honor or capitalize on the event. Other noted dates of seemingly equal importance, such as Columbus Day, have produced few associated collectibles.

Symbolic of the "Glorious Fourth" is Uncle Sam, who has become a personification of the spirit of the American people. Lithographed paper and cardboard candy containers in this form were sold by the Fanny Farmer chain of candy stores. Dating from 1930–50, the piece was manufactured in the United States. It is 6″ high, and the jointed arms indicate that it was probably designed to be used also as a toy.

Independence Day

First celebrated on July 8, 1776, four days after the actual signing of the Declaration of Independence, the "Glorious Fourth" soon became a nationwide event marked by parades, dinners, patriotic speeches by politicians and public figures of every stripe, and, of course, every imaginable form of fireworks display. The parades and speeches continue, as do the celebratory fireworks, though the latter are greatly curtailed by laws designed to prevent the horrendous number of deaths and injuries that in the nineteenth century were accepted as "part of the price one pays for freedom."

Types of Fourth of July Collectibles

The two major categories of Independence Day artifacts center on the small decorative figures used at the dinner table and the packages in which firecrackers, Roman candles, and other fireworks are shipped and sold. Toys related to the event are also fairly common.

Candy containers and favors The Fourth of July banquet table was—and sometimes still is—festooned with favors, some of which served also as candy containers. Figures of Uncle Sam are especially common, as he has come to personify the government and people of the United States. Though in essence his name is a play on the initials "U.S.," the traditional figure, which first appeared in the 1850s, has come to be associated with one "Uncle" Samuel Wilson (1766–1854), of Troy, New York. Wilson served as a government meat inspector at the time of the War of 1812, and the initials "U.S." on casks of beef became associated both with him and with the national image.

Most Uncle Sam figurines are small, less than six inches tall, and made either of lithographed paper and cardboard, or of papier-mâché or plaster of

OPPOSITE: *Perhaps one of the most popular collectibles associated with the celebration of independence is the "Hero of '76," a lithographed paper and painted-wood jointed figure manufactured around 1876 by the Charles M. Crandall Company of Pennsylvania. Designed to represent a soldier of the Continental Army, the piece could serve either as a toy or as a table decoration.*

Paris, in each case sometimes with the traditional tails and striped pants in cloth. The earliest common examples are German, dating from the 1920s, but there are also American ones from the 1940–60 period. Nodding-head pieces are found but must be considered rare.

Other favors include candy containers in the form of top hats such as Uncle Sam wears, and a variety of boxes either designed to look like a firecracker or decorated with imitation firecrackers. In one such specimen, what appears to be a firecracker wick turns out to be, upon withdrawal, a fanlike American flag of tissue paper.

Greeting cards Well into the twentieth century it was customary for some people to send Fourth of July greetings. Most of these were in the form of penny postcards, which may be found in sufficient variety to allow for a large and interesting collection.

Other paper goods associated with the date include tablecloths and napkins with brightly printed decoration, and the elaborate programs often issued to commemorate Independence Day events. The latter may be of considerable local historical interest and are of primary concern to museums, libraries, and historical societies.

Toys Most common of playthings associated with this holiday are the cast-iron cannons used in firing salutes to the Glorious Fourth. The smaller ones (up to six inches) were usually designed to accommodate a firecracker, but larger cannons fired black powder charges. These pieces might be two feet long, and they could be extremely dangerous. Overloaded or defective cannons frequently burst, causing injuries or even death. Nevertheless, they were very popular, and numerous examples have survived.

Related toys included hundreds of different cast-iron cap guns and "bombs" in which paper gunpowder caps could be exploded. Cap guns had a hammer mechanism like a real pistol, while the "bombs" were thrown into the air, causing a cap to explode when they landed on a hard surface. Most popular are the so-called animated cap pistols, which had figures incorporated into their design. When the trigger was pulled, a cap would explode and the figures would react: one man would, for example, kick another. Although both cap guns and bombs were used year round by children, they were most popular on the Fourth.

There were less noisy toys, such as the jointed, wood and lithographed paper "Hero of '76," a patriotic plaything created at the time of the 1876

This painted papier-mâché head of Uncle Sam sports a lithographed paper and cardboard hat, pipe-cleaner goatee and sideburns. It is 2″ in diameter, and the pipe-cleaner "legs" indicate that the piece was probably a cake or table decoration. The lithographed paper and cardboard top hat doubles as a candy container; it is 4.5″ high. Both pieces were made in Germany, c. 1930–40.

ABOVE LEFT: *The bright colors and amusing scene on this "Noi-Zee Boy" label typify the characteristics that appeal to a growing army of firecracker-label collectors. Dating to the 1950s, the label measures 5" by 8" and was made in Macau of lithographed paper.* ABOVE RIGHT: *This 5" by 8" "Yan Kee Boy" brick label was produced in Macau, c. 1930–40. The label is of lithographed paper.*

Centennial by the Charles M. Crandall Company of Montrose, Pennsylvania. It depicted a Continental soldier saluting the American flag. Found also are board games incorporating a patriotic theme such as "Old Glory," "Yankee Doodle," and "Uncle Sam," all produced prior to 1900 by Parker Brothers of Salem, Massachusetts.

Folk art Folk art associated with the Fourth of July includes innumerable representations of Uncle Sam. Some are whirligigs or small mantel carvings; particularly popular are the life-size painted and saw-cut Uncle Sam mailbox holders, which stand by the hundreds along rural and suburban roads. Though a few are earlier, the majority of these are almost contemporary since they were made in honor of the Bicentennial in 1976.

Fireworks memorabilia A new and rapidly expanding area of Independence Day memorabilia encompasses labels from the packets and boxes in which firecrackers and other fireworks came, as well as the mail-order catalogues in which these were advertised. The brightly lithographed labels are particularly appealing and, unlike many collectibles, remain inexpensive. While most enthusiasts favor labels and fireworks from American manufacturers, numerous examples produced in Hong Kong or Taiwan may be found.

Vigil lamps Mirroring the tradition established on the first Independence Day when candles were placed in the windows of Philadelphia homes, nineteenth-century Americans placed colored, molded-glass vigil lamps in their windows. In 1876, John R. Shirley of Providence, Rhode Island, advertised these in red, green, and blue, as well as clear glass, at $1.50 per dozen. Unlike similar Christmas lamps which hung on trees, these were flat-bottomed so they might stand on a window sill. They are rarely found today.

An early brick label for Camel Brand salutes, dating to the 1930s. It is of lithographed paper, 4" by 8", and was made in Macau or Hong Kong.

Martha Washington was the most popular spouse of any early president, and her picture often appears with that of our nation's father. Here they adorn a 1930s, 10″ china plate, which was manufactured at an American pottery.

Washington's Birthday

February 22, the birth date of George Washington, acknowledged "Father of his Country," was first celebrated in 1778 when the Comte de Rochambeau, Commander-in-Chief of the French forces supporting the American cause, declared a holiday, and Proctor's Artillery Band, one of the numerous musical groups accompanying the troops, held forth in concert. Following Washington's death in 1799 the holiday quickly assumed national importance second only to that of Independence Day, though it has always been of a more solemn nature and for decades was observed almost as a day of mourning.

Types of Washington's Birthday Collectibles

Dinners, both public and private, were central to the celebration of Washington's Birthday, and the favors and candy boxes used at these are popular with collectors. Postcards sent to mark the occasion are also sought after, as are various folk paintings and sculpture commemorating the event.

Favors and candy containers The favors and candy boxes placed at each location on the table for the Washington's Birthday dinner were of two general types. There were representations of the general, either full figure, sometimes mounted on horseback, or a bust. And there were small hatchets, tree stumps, or combinations of the two. These, of course, were an allusion to the legend of Washington's having as a youth cut down a family cherry tree and then confessed to the act after stating that "I cannot tell a lie." The whole story, however, was a lie—a tale concocted years after Washington's death by one Parson Weems.

In any case, the papier-mâché or composition hatchets and stumps, most of which open at one end for the insertion of sugar candies, are appealing collectibles. Also of interest are the carefully molded representations of the first President. Usually of composition or plaster of Paris, these may be free-

standing or mounted on a drumlike candy box of cardboard.
As with Christmas, Easter, and Halloween examples, these favors
might come in sets with a large (often 12″–18″ high) centerpiece
and a dozen or more smaller specimens for individual placement.

One more traditional object found at the table was the chocolate
disc wrapped in foil to mimic the silver dollar Washington is alleged
to have thrown across the Potomac. Another dubious story this—and
due to their perishable nature, the chocolate dollars are about as rare
as the original silver one.

RIGHT: *Given the contemporary penchant for holidays adjusted to
vacationers' convenience, it is hard to imagine the patriotic enthusiasm that once surrounded the celebration of Washington's Birthday.
Public banquets, common during the nineteenth century, were later
replaced by private gatherings at which each table was decorated
with favors such as the candy box seen here. Made of plaster of
Paris, printed paper, and cardboard, the figure of our
nation's first president is 3″ high. He bears an iron-
wire sword, and the base opens to allow insertion of sugar sweets. Made in Germany c.
1920–35.*

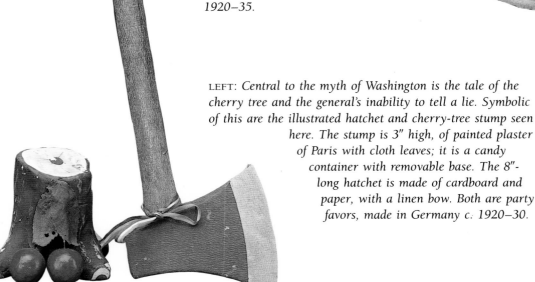

LEFT: *Central to the myth of Washington is the tale of the
cherry tree and the general's inability to tell a lie. Symbolic
of this are the illustrated hatchet and cherry-tree stump seen
here. The stump is 3″ high, of painted plaster
of Paris with cloth leaves; it is a candy
container with removable base. The 8″-
long hatchet is made of cardboard and
paper, with a linen bow. Both are party
favors, made in Germany c. 1920–30.*

OPPOSITE: *This finely cast pair of painted George Washington andirons was manufactured in the eastern United States c. 1900–10. Each is 13″ tall and retains
most of the original paint. Other patriotic andirons include representations of
Liberty, the American eagle, and Columbia.*

Washington's death in 1799 was a profound shock to his countrymen and led to the creation of various forms of memorial art. This nineteenth-century view of Mount Vernon and Washington's tomb alongside the Potomac River was done in charcoal on paper covered with ground marble, a technique we now refer to as "sandpaper painting." Measuring 14" by 20", the piece is from the eastern United States.

Greeting cards Greetings are still exchanged on Washington's Birthday, but the custom was much more common sixty years ago. A certain number of such cards designed to be mailed in envelopes will be seen, but most were of the penny-postal variety.

Folk art Sculpture and paintings of our nation's first chief of state abound. Among the former are not only folk carvings in a charmingly naive manner but also more formal representations such as the pair of cast andirons shown here. However, among the art most closely associated with Washington are memorial paintings and needleworks made to commemorate his death. These are done in several mediums, and usually incorporate a tomb with mourners (often including Columbia and a wounded veteran), a weeping willow tree, and perhaps a representation of Mount Vernon. Such works were sometimes done by young women for presentation to their parents on Washington's Birthday.

114

*Though once exchanged in great numbers, Washington's Birthday greeting cards
are seldom seen today. This postcard was printed in Germany c. 1910–30.*

Lincoln's Birthday

Second only to Washington in the hierarchy of national figures is Abraham Lincoln, the "Great Emancipator." His birthday, February 12, is especially honored among black Americans. However, celebration of the date has never reached the extremes of enthusiasm shown for Washington's Birthday, and the number of related collectibles is minimal.

Greeting cards As with Washington, it was at one time customary to send greeting cards, usually of the penny-postal sort, to friends and family on Lincoln's Birthday. These often featured a lithographed picture of Abe, with some lines from his Emancipation Proclamation.

Folk art Folk paintings and carvings of Lincoln were frequently made to be displayed in the home either year round or at the time of his birthday. There are even a few whirligigs featuring the Great Emancipator.

OPPOSITE: *Despite his impact on American history, fewer objects associated with Abraham Lincoln are found, probably because in the South he remains a controversial figure even today. Nevertheless, his birthday is celebrated, especially among blacks, one of whom, Elijah Pierce (b. 1892), created this painted relief carving around 1975. It measures 14.5" by 9.25" and was made in Ohio.*

RIGHT: *Representations of the founding fathers need not be severe. The New Jersey folk sculptor Janice Fenimore (b. 1924) created this humorous whirligig of Abe Lincoln in 1978. The painted wood and tin figure measures 22.5" in height. Its finely sculpted features and detailed dress make this piece particularly appealing to collectors.*

117

Columbus Day

The discovery of the New World by Christopher Columbus in 1492 is commemorated in the United States each October 12. The unquestioned importance of this event is reflected not only in the traditional parades but also in a few collectible objects. Chief among these are greeting cards, including the penny-postal sort, which were exchanged on the date. There is also a single plaything: a cast-iron bell toy representing the great discoverer in the prow of his ship. When the toy was pulled along the floor, a large bell would ring.

Manufacturers

Patriotic collectibles were made almost exclusively in this country or in Germany for export here. Cast-iron playthings such as cannons, cap guns, and wheel toys were manufactured by such well-known nineteenth- and early-twentieth-century American firms as E. R. Ives & Co. of Bridgeport, Connecticut, the Kenton Hardware Company located in the Ohio community of the same name, and J. & E. Stevens of Cromwell, Connecticut. Patriotic games were turned out by Parker Brothers of Salem, Massachusetts, and McLoughlin Brothers of New York.

A few American firms have produced cardboard and papier-mâché favors and candy boxes, particularly during the 1930–60 period; but the great majority of these, especially the finer examples, were turned out by the same German firms that made similar items for other holidays such as Halloween and Christmas. Marks appear on some pieces but most are left unmarked.

Again, until the onset of World War II (with a hiatus during the 1914–18 period), practically all patriotic post- and envelope cards sold in this country were printed in Germany. After 1945 American printers dominated the market, but by that time the demand for such cards had dwindled. German greeting cards usually are plainly marked as to country of origin.

OPPOSITE: *Few collectibles are associated with Columbus Day; however, this painted cast-iron pull toy would fall into that category. The ship is embossed* LANDING OF COLUMBUS, *and the discoverer stands in the bow. A bell rings as the piece rolls across the floor. Approximately 5" by 7", this toy was made c. 1905 by the J. & E. Stevens Company of Cromwell, Connecticut.*

OTHER HOLIDAYS

*C*ertain holidays, though of great importance to many people, have either not yet attracted much collector interest or have not generated a large number of collectible objects. These areas remain relatively untouched, offering new and promising fields to the enterprising collector.

Hanukkah

In the Jewish faith the celebration of Hanukkah, the Festival of Lights, occurs on the 25th of Kislev (in December). According to a Talmudic legend, when the priests reentered the Temple desecrated by Antiochus Epiphanes they could find but a single small container of unpolluted oil for the holy lanterns. Miraculously, though, this lasted eight days, until a new supply could be obtained.

Accordingly, in 165 B.C. the feast of Hanukkah was instituted by the Maccabees to commemorate the rededication of the Temple. Central to the holiday is the lighting of the eight-branched candlestick or menorah. According to the Shammaite or older tradition, all eight candles or founts are lit the first night; they are then reduced by one on each following night. The later Hillelites lit a single light the first night and added another on each succeeding evening. Traditionally, there are as many candlestands or oil lamps as there are entrances to the home.

Not surprisingly, the most collectible objects from this holiday are the Hanukkah lamps or candelabra, which may be found in great variety. Some are of precious metal, others of pottery or tin.

Gifts are given and games played during the period of Hanukkah, and a traditional toy, the dreidel or top, is given to children. These tops, too, are collectible. They are found in wood, both painted and unpainted, in metal, and in pottery.

May Day

Though now thought of primarily as a labor event with heavy political overtones, May Day is a holiday of great antiquity, traceable to Roman and Druidic customs. The traditional European celebration involved three interrelated phases. The first of these was the gathering, on Walpurgis Day Eve (April 30), of flowers and greens with which the doors and windows of each home were decorated. This "going a-Maying" or "bringing in the May" symbolized the bringing of new life into the village.

On the following day, May 1, a Maypole was set up in the village square, decorated with flowers and ribbons, and all joined in a communal dance about it. Presiding over the festivities was the May Queen, who was popularly chosen and who might lead a procession through the community, sometimes soliciting alms to fund the festivities.

The importance of May Day is reflected in the many beliefs and superstitions surrounding it. These include washing in the "May dew" before sunrise to improve both one's complexion and one's luck; the idea that Mayflowers, also picked before sunrise, will prevent freckles; that if you look down a well this day you will see your future spouse's face; and that getting your head wet in the rain will prevent headache during the coming year.

In the United States, children until well into the 1930s not only danced about the Maypole but also made May baskets of cardboard covered with brightly covered paper. These were filled with wildflowers and left as gifts at the doors of neighbors. These baskets as well as Maypole decorations offer opportunities for the diligent collector. Greeting cards were also sent on May Day, and a significant variety is available.

St. Patrick's Day

Initially celebrated only in Ireland, St. Patrick's Day has become an important holiday in the United States, joined in by most Americans regardless of religion or national origin. The legend of St. Patrick is a long and complex one involving the saint's kidnapping by Irish pirates, years of enslavement in Ireland during which he became a Christian, escape and the taking of priestly vows and, finally, a triumphant return in A.D. 432 to the Emerald Isle in the course of which he converted the populace and drove out all the snakes.

The American St. Patrick's Day was first celebrated in Boston by members of the Charitable Irish Society on March 17, 1737. The traditional date has been maintained to this time. The main events of the day consist of a parade, a Catholic mass, and a family dinner.

It is with the last that most collectibles are associated. These consist primarily of the cardboard or papier-mâché candy containers or favors (usually German made) that graced each place at the table. They may be in the form of an Irishman, a group of Irish children in festive dress, a top hat, or even a pig—evoking the legend of "Paddy's pig." Also seen are representations of the leprechaun, a small, mischievous elf who supposedly always has a hoard of buried treasure.

St. Patrick's Day collectibles center on the traditional family dinner. Seen here are two candy containers. The first is of cardboard and lithographed paper in the form of a bottle of the well-known Irish whiskey; it is 5.5" high. The cork may be removed to insert candy. The traditional Kelly green top hat is filled from the bottom and is only 3" tall. The clay pipe and wire and silk thread shamrock are both closely associated with Ireland and with the holiday. Both these pieces are from the 1930–40 period.

This St. Patrick's Day postcard was printed by the well-known Raphael Tuck & Sons of London, c. 1925–35.

All these forms may be decorated with symbols associated with the Irish and the holiday: the long-stemmed clay pipe, the horseshoe that is thought to bring good luck and repel evil, and the clover, the national emblem of Ireland. The last is always worn on St. Patrick's Day, as the saint used it to illustrate the mystery of the Trinity. In fact, the expression "to drown the Shamrock" refers to the custom of going from tavern to tavern drinking holiday toasts.

St. Patrick's Day greeting cards date from the early 1900s and are still popular. Until the 1930s, most were of the penny-postal variety; today, envelope cards are the norm, and humorous topics are customary. American manufacturers such as Hallmark now dominate the field, though most early examples were produced in Germany.

Mardi Gras

The Mardi Gras of New Orleans is but a single manifestation of the great carnivals that take place each year in many European and Latin American nations and, especially, in Mexico, Argentina, and Brazil. Although in most cases greatly commercialized today, these rituals combine Christian traditions (*carne vale,* or "flesh farewell," reflects the last secular indulgence before the onset of Lent) with pagan ceremonies centered on the expulsion of winter and demons harmful to the coming crops.

Memorabilia associated with Mardi Gras relate to the central features of the holiday: the great parades or processionals, and the masquerade balls. Both involve elaborate costumes and headdresses, and these are sought by a limited number of sophisticated collectors. However, since they are so prized that they may be handed down from generation to generation, it is often difficult to obtain earlier examples. On the other hand, it is not hard to obtain the favors handed out at Mardi Gras balls and dinners, the dance programs, and other ephemera associated with the event. These too are of interest to many.

While the items described here are the ones most commonly found, they represent but a portion of holiday-related collectibles. Enthusiasts may seek out many others, such as the souvenir coins issued to commemorate the centennials or bicentennials of American towns and states, and the illustrated booklets and programs issued as mementos of these events. There are many state and local holidays and most produce some sort of collectible. It is just a matter of discovering what piques your interest.

Glossary of Terms

Bisque: Unglazed porcelain with a matte finish, made from kaolin clay and other ingredients, and usually lightly tinted, at least in part.

Blown glass: Glassware shaped by blowing air into molten glass, employing a metal blowpipe and various forming tools.

Celluloid: A highly flammable compound of cellulose nitrate and camphor introduced in 1870 and employed in toy- and dollmaking through the 1930s.

Chalkware: Molded and painted ornamental figures made from processed gypsum and water.

Composition: A mixture of paper and wood pulp, similar to papier-mâché but containing additional ingredients such as sawdust or plaster.

Crepe paper: Thin, colored paper stretched and crimped. Its crinkled surface adds a different dimension to holiday decorations.

Embossed: Raised in relief from the surface by molding or stamping; commonly used in decorating greeting cards.

Ephemera: A collectors' term used to designate objects such as post- and greeting cards, posters and newspapers, which are so fragile as to be easily destroyed if not carefully handled.

Flocking: Thin fuzzy or velvety fibers of wool or felt glued to a surface to mimic hair, fur, or similar substances.

Gilded: Covered with a thinly applied coat of gold paint or gold leaf.

Lithography: Mechanical process involving printing from a flat stone or metal plate onto paper, wood, or other materials.

Mark: An identifying cipher placed on a product by its manufacturer. Marks may be embossed, impressed, incised, or applied with ink, usually in the form of a stamp.

Molded: Cast for form in a metal or plaster mold made in the desired shape. Liquid is poured into the mold, or a semi-solid material such as composition is pressed into it.

Papier-mâché: A mixture of paper pulp, glue, and sometimes chalk or sand that, once molded, dries to a hard mass which can be cut with a saw and painted.

Plastic: Any of several compounds produced from organic components and capable of being molded into various forms and hardened.

Spun glass: Fine glass fiber formed by shaping liquid glass into a thread.

Bibliography

BOOKS

Baur, John, *Christmas on the American Frontier*. Caldwell, Idaho: Caxton Printers, 1961.

Brenner, Robert, *Christmas Revisited*. West Chester, Pa.: Schiffer Publishing Ltd., 1986.

Davis, Hubert, *Christmas in the Mountains*. Murfreesboro, N.C.: Johnson Publishing Co., 1972.

Engle, Paul, *Prairie Christmas*. New York: Lowsmans & Green, 1960.

Gray, Nada, *Holidays Victorian Women Celebrate in Pennsylvania*. Lewisburg, Pa.: Union County Historical Society, n.d.

Leach, Maria, *Dictionary of Folklore, Mythology and Legend* (2 vols.). New York: Funk & Wagnalls, 1949.

Rogers, Maggie, and Hawkins, Judith, *The Glass Christmas Ornament: Old and New*. Forest Grove, Ore.: Timber Press, 1977.

————, and Hallinan, Peter R., *The Santa Claus Picture Book*. New York: E. P. Dutton, 1980.

Schiffer, Margaret, *Holiday Toys and Decorations*. West Chester, Pa.: Schiffer Publishing Ltd., 1985.

————, *Christmas Ornaments, A Festive Study*. West Chester, Pa.: Schiffer Publishing Ltd., 1984.

Snyder, Phillip V., *The Christmas Tree Book*. New York: Viking Press, 1976.

Stille, Eva, *Christbaumschmuck*. Nuremberg, West Germany: Hans Carl, 1983.

ARTICLES

Bane, Reynolds, "The Decorated Egg from Hobby to Art," *The Antiques Journal* (May 1980).

Boyer, Pam, "Christmas Light Bulbs," *The Antiques Journal* (December 1976).

Bryan-Smith, Lissa, "Collecting the Merry Men of Christmas," *New York-Pennsylvania Collector* (December 1987).

———, "At Home with a Turkey," *New York-Pennsylvania Collector* (October 1987).

Cassidy, Ina Sizer, "Christmas in New Mexico," *El Palacio* (December 1950).

Gilbert, Anne, "Putz: Tree-Trimming, Pennsylvania-Dutch Style," *New York-Pennsylvania Collector* (December 1987).

Hallenberg, Heather, "Cincinnati Collects Christmas," *Antiques Review* (December 1987).

Hallmark Cards, Inc., ed., "British Businessman Began Christmas Card Traditions," *New York-Pennsylvania Collector* (December 1987).

Heilbron, Bertha L., "Christmas and New Year's on the Frontier," *Minnesota History* (December 1935).

Krythe, Maymie R., "Daily Life in Early Los Angeles, Part II, Holiday Celebrations," Historical Society of Southern California *Quarterly* (June 1954).

Pullar, Elizabeth, "May Day Customs," *The Antiques Journal* (May 1980).

———, "Old Valentine Fashions," *The Antiques Journal* (February 1981).

Russo, Angelo M., "Season's Greetings," *Antiques and the Arts Weekly* (December 25, 1987).

Shuart, Harry Wilson, "Made in America Christmas Tree Ornaments," *Spinning Wheel* (January–February 1975).

———, "Christmas Lights," *Spinning Wheel* (December 1973).

———, "Glass Christmas Tree Ornaments," *Spinning Wheel* (January–February 1978).

———, "The German Easter Toy Parade," *Spinning Wheel* (April 1972).

Walker, Norman M., "The Holidays in Early Louisiana," *Magazine of American History* (December 1883).

Witter, Evelyn, "How Santa Gained Weight," *The Antiques Journal* (December 1973).

A NOTE ON THE TYPE

The text of this book was set in ITC Berkeley Old Style which was based on the Frederic W. Goudy (1865–1947) type designed in 1938 for the University of California Press. It was issued to the trade in 1959 by Lanston Monotype as Californian. The International Typeface Corporation version was brought out in 1983.

The California type was the climax of Goudy's fifty-year career. This prolific American designer cut many well-known types such as Copperplate Gothic, Deepdene, Hadriano, Kennerley, Pabst, and, of course, those bearing his name.

Composed by Sarabande Press, New York, New York
Color separations, printing, and binding by
Martin Cook Associates, Hong Kong
Designed by Virginia Tan